A Simple
CELEBRATION

A·SIMPLE
CELEBRATION

A VEGETARIAN COOKBOOK
FOR BODY, MIND, AND SPIRIT

■ *The Nutritional Program From* ■

THE CHOPRA CENTER FOR WELL BEING

Ginna Bell Bragg AND *David Simon, M.D.*

A Simple
CELEBRATION

A Vegetarian Cookbook for Body, Mind, and Spirit

The Nutritional Program
from The
Chopra Center for Well Being

Ginna Bell Bragg and David Simon, M.D.

Foreword by Deepak Chopra, M.D.

Three Rivers Press/New York

Published by Three Rivers Press, a division of Crown Publishers, Inc., 201 East 50th Street, New York, New York 10022. Member of the Crown Publishing Group.

Originally published in hardcover by Harmony Books, 1997

Random House, Inc. New York, Toronto, London, Sydney, Auckland
www.randomhouse.com

THREE RIVERS PRESS and colophon are trademarks of Crown Publishers, Inc.

Printed in the United States of America

Design by Lynne Amft

Library of Congress Cataloging-in-Publication Data
Bragg, Ginna Bell.
   A simple celebration : a vegetarian cookbook for body, mind, and spirit : the nutritional program from the Chopra Center for Well Being / Ginna Bell Bragg and David Simon : foreword by Deepak Chopra. — 1st paperback ed.
Originally published : New York : Harmony Books, ©1997
Includes index.
   1. Vegetarian cookery. 2. Medicine, Ayurvedic. I. Simon, David. II. Title.
   [TX837.B74 1998]   97-48373
   641.5'636—dc21   CIP

ISBN 0-609-80181-3

10 9 8 7 6 5 4 3 2 1

First Paperback Edition

To Sister Mary Helen, O.P., who opened my mind; to Sister Mary Augustine, O.P., who planted my feet on a creative path; and to Sister Mary Burns, O.P., who gave me wings.

God Bless You.

G.B.B.

A C K N O W L E D G M E N T S

My first thanks must go posthumously to my parents, Virginia and Richard Bragg, both artists, whose union provided the mix of chromosomes that created me. Thank you for your undying love, even now;

to my son, Michael, whose management, hugs, and cups of tea have sustained me;

to my dear friends Ken Gregg, Fred Coleman, Sampson Bowers, Rachel Coleman, and Rick Dinihanian, all of whom provided money, loyalty, and encouragement to bring me to this moment;

to my brothers, Mark and Jess Bragg, and my lovely sisters-in-law, Pegge and Patty, whose devotion and kind words know no bounds;

to my girlfriends Nan Heflin, Mary Kay Fry, and Toni Ahlgren, whose wonder at and joy of life gave me constant courage to go on; and John Lyle, dear companion;

to Caroline Graham Muir, who introduced me to Bragg's Liquid Aminos, and the rest is history;

to John Gladstein and his mountaintop Rainbow Ranch, my starting point;

to Muriel Nellis, agent extraordinaire, and to Shaye Areheart, our editor, Dina Siciliano, her assistant, and all the good people at Harmony Books, for their knowledge and support;

to Barbara St. George, Mary Horner, and Johnathan Copen-haver, my original Center staff, for their faithful observance of kitchen consciousness; and Chris Saxon Barley, whose assistance in service, photographs, and transcriptions was invaluable;

to my most conscious spiritual advisors, Revs. Joan Gattuso and Jane Meyers, whose over-the-phone meditations and guidance brought peace into my heart at the most intense moments, and whose example as spiritual beings encourages me to "walk my talk";

to David, who saw me, knew me, and gave light to this book;

to Peter, who just plain loves me;

to Deepak, for inspiration;

and to Great Spirit, for the gift of this life.

Namasté.

Ginna Bell Bragg

My love and appreciation flow to the many celestial souls who have provided me with love and nourishment along my journey:

to my mother and father, Lee Shirley and Myron, for their unconditional nurturing;

to my cherished family, Howard, Dana, and Samantha, for their unconditional sharing;

to my beloved son, Max, for his unconditional mirroring;

to Pamela, for her unconditional love;

to my many dear friends and colleagues at The Chopra Center for Well Being and Infinite Possibilities International, for their commitment to the embodiment of Spirit;

to the Divine Mother incarnation, Ginna, for her culinary alchemy;

and to my dear friend, brother, and teacher, Deepak, for his unwavering pursuit of the miraculous.

Love and light,

David Simon

CONTENTS

FOREWORD

"Food is Brahman," proclaim the ancient Vedic texts. Brahman is consciousness, and the physical body that we inhabit for the time being is condensed consciousness. The mind is a field of ideas. The body is a field of molecules. One is consciousness in thought form, the other is consciousness in material form, but the two are aspects of the same field of pure intelligence in different disguises.

Consciousness curving back within itself creates ego, intellect, mind, the physical body, and the experience of the material world. This, declare the great sages, is the process through which the seer becomes the scenery, the observer becomes the observed, and the creator becomes the creation. Creator and creation are one. Food is Brahman.

You may look at an item of food and see only its color and form, experience only its texture or taste. But food is an expression of the same universal mind that creates your body and has the same levels of manifestation that comprise your physical form. Ayurvedic texts declare that you have a physical body made up of matter and energy, a subtle body made up of mind, intellect, and ego, and a causal body made up of soul and spirit. When you look at a banana or a glass of orange juice, you may not fully grasp that there is *prana*, or universal energy, there, or that the same spirit that animates everything that lives, moves, or breathes exists in food, but it's there all the same.

From the state of being we begin to experience the material universe as our extended body. Then nature is no longer something to be conquered, subjugated, and exploited. When we are ready to have an intimate relationship with the womb of creation that is Mother Earth, we will be healed. More than anything else, modern nutrition needs to understand that food is not mere calories, proteins, fats, minerals, and vitamins. Food is intelligence. We are intelligence and we are in constant and dynamic exchange with universal intelligence through physiological processes, of which eating is the most important. Eating, digestion, and metabolism are the transformation of one mode of intelligence into another. The life energy in a kernel of corn today may become a light receptor in your eye tomorrow, which decodes the intelligence of the universe into color and form. When we understand the miracle of life and begin to comprehend that life feeds upon itself to transform itself into different manifestations, we will begin to have some insight into the magic and miracle of living. Life is a miracle. Eating is a miracle. We begin as a speck of information on a DNA molecule, food is added, and that same food is transformed into our brain, intellect, and ego, which begins to ask itself: "Who am I? Where do I come from? What is the meaning of my existence?"

All the great wisdom traditions of the world have looked upon the miracle of nutrition as something sacred. If we could understand this one idea —that the Absolute (spirit) transforms itself into the Relative (physical world) through its own self-sacrifice—eating would be elevated to the stature of a sacrament. When we develop reverence for food and the miracle of transformation inherent in it, just the simple act of eating creates a ritual of celebration. This is what we really need in our awareness—to make eating a celebration. Every disease that humans are prey to, from cardiovascular problems to cancer to degenerative disorders, has been linked in some way or another to diet. Despite this understanding, our approach to diet to date has been clinical, sterile, and void of the mystery of life that is present in every act of eating. Modern nutritional science looks at food as a dead substance that can be quantified in calories and described by its biochemical constituents. A vast number of our population is sustained by so-called nutrients that are imprisoned for extended periods of time in cans or frozen packages. There is no life energy in eating this food, but science smugly declares that it contains everything our bodies need. As long as our approach to life is technical, we will remain mere technicians. Our physicians are no longer healers but great technicians who know almost everything about the human body but practically nothing about the human soul. We require a transformation that can only be called holy. We need to transform the way we look at life itself and in that transformation we will remember that food, too, has a soul.

This book is about food for the soul. It is about the celebration of nourishment at all levels: physical, mental, and spiritual. It is about wholeness and therefore about healing and that which is holy.

Ingest the knowledge in this book and digest it as you would a sumptuous meal and you will participate consciously in the cosmic dance of transformation. Every moment is full of energy, vitality, awareness, and joy.

DEEPAK CHOPRA, M.D.

INTRODUCTION

Open Heart, Open Mind

GINNA: I love food and I love to cook. I love shopping for special ingredients, meeting local farmers and bakers, growing succulent vegetables, and creating beautiful, health-supporting meals. When I first began my exploration of Ayurvedic cooking, I was deeply moved by the reverence this ancient healing system has for the value of nutritious food and the person who lovingly prepares it. The principle that nourishment comes from the love of the cook as well as the food on your plate completely resonated with my beliefs and experience.

DAVID: I love food and I love to eat. When I first tasted Ginna's fabulous cooking, I was delighted because I could actually taste the flavor of love in her food. I was so inspired that I recruited her to prepare the meals for our program at The Chopra Center for Well Being.

GINNA: I was merrily cooking for retreats and workshops in northern California, living in a 400-square-foot tepee, when David came along with his taste buds. I was practicing Ayurvedic principles in my kitchen—arising early, meditating, beginning each day with beautiful chants, music, and the aroma of my favorite incense. The guests arriving for breakfast frequently commented on the healing and nourishing energy they received, even *before* they put food in their mouths.

DAVID: This makes sense because according to Ayurveda, the universe is a magnificent and magical web of energy and information. Each of our lives is a unique and dynamic design within the cosmic weaving. Our thoughts and feelings extend across time and space, so Ginna's consciousness and caring are tangible in and around her food.

GINNA: My true dharma, or purpose in life, is providing sustenance and nourishment for people along their path of spiritual growth. Nutritionally supporting and educating people at The Chopra Center for Well Being provide the opportunity to serve others while expressing my unique talents.

DAVID: When people make a commitment to transform and improve their lives, it is often reflected in their food choices. Whether you are recovering from an illness, changing jobs or relationships, or simply want to "live healthier," food provides a tangible way to demonstrate your change. This book is dedicated to supporting and celebrating your progress on the path of increasing happiness and wholeness.

GINNA: My intention in collaborating on this book is not only to share recipes and ingredients, but to explore with you the spiritual and mindful aspects of cooking. To paraphrase Picasso, when I enter the kitchen, I leave my concerns outside the door, like a Moslem who removes his shoes before entering the mosque. In other words, I surrender to the task, giving my heart and soul to the preparation of a delicious meal. In this state, the cook, the preparation, and the meal itself are seen as different expressions of the same creative force, motivated by love and the impulse to nourish.

DAVID: One of the important goals of this book is to demonstrate that it is easy to prepare delicious food that is enjoyable by Westerners and fully resonates with the principles of Ayurveda. We do not need to eat curries at every meal in order to enjoy a balanced, health-enhancing diet. The ancient mind body principles of Ayurveda can be readily applied to dishes from every culture.

DAVID AND GINNA: We offer this book as an expression of our love. We hope it will inspire you to share your love through the preparation of food, whether it is for yourself or others. Preparing and sharing delicious and nutritious food is a celebration of both our uniqueness and our unity.

Chapter

1

HEART AND SOUL OF THE COOK

KITCHEN CONSCIOUSNESS— COOKING WITH LOVE

The artistic spirit in us all craves attractive surroundings, which inspire us to bring forth beautiful creations. Whatever we focus on in our lives—be it painting, writing, making music, or cooking—there is a wonderful benefit to wrapping ourselves in warm, inviting, inspiring settings with comfortable chairs, healthy plants, beautiful music, and the right books. Prop your feet up on the desk to read cookbooks; curl up in front of the fire to write down recipes.

The kitchen can be your studio for creating nourishing, beautiful meals for yourself and your family and friends. You don't need to be an artist or a professional cook to prepare fabulous food. All you need are fresh ingredients, a selection of herbs and spices, a sharp knife, and love.

Love is the essential ingredient. It is the channel through which every good meal flows. Whether as cooks at home or as professional chefs, we are cooking to nourish the human race. When we contribute to the health, well-being, and happiness of one individual, we are contributing to the health, well-being, and happiness of the whole planet.

Every time someone eats a meal cooked with your love, they carry away with them a fuller heart and a more lively spirit. You are offering your best to those who can benefit from your love and attention.

Love of food begins with love of life. Ayurveda tells us that "food is Brahman." Brahman is pure potentiality. We are not only what we eat, we are the thoughts that go into what we eat. If what we eat has been cooked by an angry, hostile person, we ultimately take away with us their anger and hostility and give it back to the world. If we eat food prepared by someone filled with love and caring, these ingredients fill our body, mind, and soul. Then we find it easiest to share the best of ourselves with those around us.

Ayurveda teaches us that the most satisfying and nourishing meals come from farmers who grow their crops with love, grocers who sell their produce with love, and preparers who cook with love. Even if you cannot personally meet your food growers, choose your materials carefully, remembering that each ingredient is an essential part of the whole of your creation. If you begin with good whole ingredients, your salads will be fresher, your vegetable dishes more succulent, and your breads more nourishing.

Whenever possible, we recommend the use of organic, locally grown produce but it may not always be possible to find it in your market. If this is the case, choose the best grains, flour, nuts, fruits, and vegetables available and cook with love.

The herbs and spices in your kitchen can make or break a meal. Beautifully cut and stir-fried vegetables can be delightful if spiced just right, or unpalatable if spiced too heavily or with the wrong flavor. As we'll discuss in the next chapter, Ayurveda teaches that different people have different constitutions. By choosing the correct herb and spice combinations, or *churans*, we can enhance each person's mind-body balance. Following the recipes in this book, we have included a Balance of Tastes Chart (page 209) to help you choose the best herbs, spices, and vegetables for your constitutional type.

According to Ayurveda, food should always be as fresh as possible. The life force, or *prana*, is most vital in meals that use fresh, recently prepared ingredients. Don't skimp when shopping for your meals. Always buy the best that is available. Day-old bread is only good for the bread crumbs you can make out of it. Use whole, beautiful, crispy vegetables and you will create the most tantalizing, savory meals.

KITCHEN TANTRA

In our Ayurvedic cooking classes at The Chopra Center for Well Being, our highest priority is the consciousness we have while cooking—our state of mind and heart while in the kitchen. We like to call this *kitchen tantra*. Tantra is a Sanskrit word that means "the fabric of life." It is the understanding that every one of our thoughts, feelings, and desires is connected to and interwoven with the whole of creation. In the West, tantra is most commonly associated with rituals of sexuality, but this is just one facet of this ancient spiritual science. A tantric approach integrates consciousness, mind, and behavior so that all our actions express our inherent spiritual nature. Kitchen tantra seeks to enliven the unity value of the cook, the cooking, and the food. In this state, the life force of the preparer merges with the life force of the food to create delicious and life-affirming meals.

Kitchen tantra is a composition in consciousness with four-part harmony. These components are *Kriya*, or ritual; *Carya*, or demeanor; *Yoga*, or integration of mind, body, and spirit; and *Anuttara*, or understanding.

Kriya (Ritual) Ritual captures our attention. Ritual in the kitchen reminds us that preparing food is a celebration of life. Perform some ritual when you are about to cook—light a candle, play music, arrange fresh flowers. Wash your hands and wipe the counter before you begin and again when you have completed the meal. Whatever you do to create your special space, to make the act of food preparation important, will contribute to the value of your meal.

Look at your kitchen as a studio designed for the creation of nourishment. Arrange your pots and pans, cooking utensils, and food products in a pleasing, accessible way, as if they were your brushes, paint tubes, and canvases. As Mother used to say, clean up as you go along and put things away in the same place each time you use them. Keep your knives sharpened, your towels clean, and your aprons fresh.

Ritual in the kitchen can be as simple as a thought—a silent mental reminder that the kitchen you enter is a holy place. See it as your temple for the joyful creation of soups, the mindful preparation of bread dough, the genesis of a celestial dessert.

Carya (Demeanor) Your kitchen can be a place of delight and your demeanor while cooking is a key ingredient in your meals. Remember to be mindful, present, and centered, focusing on the task. But don't be serious—be playful. The creative process is fun. According to Vedic knowledge, the entire universe was created for the fun of it. Cooking with a friend or beloved is a great way to express your love for each other and a fun way to play together. It also adds to the deliciousness of the meal. Be creative and open to new ideas. Trust your intuition. Be free.

Yoga (Integration) Food preparation is an opportunity to integrate body, mind, and soul. Cooking can be a moving meditation—a dance in the studio of nourishment. Meditating before you cook is a good idea, but the act of cooking itself, especially when you are alone in the kitchen, can be a satisfying meditative experience. Be an open channel for inspiration, allowing yourself to experience the pure, creative force that lies within you. When you are in a creative, meditative state in the kitchen, the magic of healing flows through you and into your soup, your pasta, and your simple fruit salads.

Anuttara (Understanding) When you bring the understanding of the masters into the kitchen, you bring balance, joy, and the spirit of celebration. The knowledge from all spiritual traditions reminds us that underlying the diversity of name and form is unity. Let this understanding of our connectedness to each other and everything in creation flow through our mind and body into our fingers as we knead the bread dough, form it into loaves, and place it in the oven. If we look at a carrot as an example of the beauty, simplicity, and perfection of the universe, we see food from the perspective of a sage, illuminated mind.

The menu, ingredients, and recipes are all important components of each meal. But your SELF is so vital to the task that you cannot for a moment lose track of it. To be conscious in the kitchen means to be fully aware of the picture of which you are a part. It is a painting in the works and you are the holder of the brush. You choose the colors, the types of paint, and the canvas. When you stand before the empty canvas, become a clear channel through which the spirit of creation flows.

Anyone who can read and shop can follow a recipe. But the consciousness of the cook, the presence of holiness in the kitchen, and the shared desire, by cook and guest, to be healthy world mates is something only love can provide. Be in love while cooking. Be love itself.

WHAT'S IN THE PANTRY?

The following is a general listing of ingredients most often used by Western cooks using Ayurvedic principles. We recommend that you always have them on hand, as so many of our recipes include them. Whenever possible, buy organic products. Refer to the Balance of Tastes Chart (page 209) for information regarding your specific constitutional needs.

Nonperishables

anise

arrowroot

asafoetida (hing)
(an Ayurvedic spice
resembling garlic)

basmati rice
(naturally grown, very
aromatic white rice)

Bragg's Liquid Aminos
(nonfermented soy sauce;
available in most natural-
food stores)

bread crumbs

buckwheat

cardamom

churans
(Vata, Pitta, Kapha)

chili paste or powder

cinnamon

cloves

coconut

coconut milk, light

coriander

corn

cumin

currants, raisins

dates

dried onion flakes

fennel seeds

flour
(organic unbleached white,
organic whole wheat
pastry, spelt)

fruit, dried

garbanzo beans
(chickpeas)

ginger, ground

honey
(pure unfiltered)

Italian seasonings

kashi
(cereal mix)

lentils
(brown, red)

maple syrup

millet

molasses

mung beans

mustard
(dry, yellow)

nutmeg

nuts and seeds

oats

olive oil

oregano

peppercorns

pine nuts

quinoa

Rice Dream

rye

sea salt

sesame oil

split peas
(yellow, green)

Sucanat
(derived from natural cane)

tarragon

thyme

tomatoes, sun-dried

turbinado sugar
(raw)

turmeric

vegetable broth powder

Vegit seasoning powder

yeast, natural

Perishables

apple juice
(unfiltered)

butter

cilantro

eggs

ghee
(clarified butter)

gingerroot, fresh

lemons

limes

milk

orange juice

Paneer cheese

parsley

tempeh

tofu

yogurt, nonfat plain

HOW, WHEN, WHAT TO BUY?

CHOOSING VEGETABLES

Buy direct from farmers whenever possible. Farmers' markets are not only valuable resources for fresh produce, they are fun, *sattvic* (creative) places to be. Most farmers love what they do, especially organic farmers who are conscious of their effect on the environment and our bodies.

Organic produce may not always look the prettiest, but it usually is the tastiest. Bruises or discolorations do not affect the flavor of the food. Look for the prominently displayed Certified Organic Grower sign. Select small fruits and vegetables, which are the most flavorful. Large zucchinis and pumpkins may look beautiful but tend to taste woody and bland. Choose delicate, young vegetables whenever possible.

GROWING YOUR OWN

Growing your own fruits and vegetables can be fun if you have the time and place. There are many wonderful books on the subject of organic gardening. Buy one that suits the area in which you live. Remember, too, to use your intuition. Plants have their own spirit that, when honored, contributes greatly to the nourishment of the meal.

SEASONS

Whether buying from the grocer or growing your own, vegetables and fruits are best eaten in season. Using locally grown produce insures that you are getting the freshest, most nutritious, and least expensive ingredients. If you do not live in a region of the country where fruits and vegetables are available year-round, purchase those that radiate the most life force. If they look and smell vital, they are most likely to taste fresh and delicious when eaten.

READING LABELS

When shopping in the grocery store, read the labels. If you can't pronounce a component, you probably don't want to eat it. Look for items that have whole ingredients, without preservatives or added salt.

CLEANING THE REFRIGERATOR

According to Ayurveda, food should be fresh, fresh, fresh. Throw out the leftovers in your refrigerator before they become science projects! No one really wants to eat them anyway. Eating food that is depleted of life force is wasting it.

NOURISHING FAMILY AND FRIENDS

Eating according to Ayurvedic principles means being more in tune with what is natural. Our society has lost this understanding because so many of us were raised on frozen meals in front of the television. People usually adapt to change if it is introduced one step at a time. Don't try to cram an Ayurvedic approach down your family's throat or you are sure to encounter resistance. The best way to influence those around you is by being an example. Begin with yourself. Prepare meals with all six tastes represented. Pay attention to the Body Intelligence Techniques (BITS) (page 18). Provide *churans* on the table for each dosha. As you begin to feel healthier and more vital, those around you will want to participate in a change that they perceive as beneficial. Relax and enjoy.

ENTERTAINING

Entertaining can be a rewarding time to express yourself artistically and Ayurvedically. Beautifully presented, balanced food feeds the soul as well as the body. Take the time to create an attractive table, using colors that enhance your menu and party theme. Even if you buy prepared food or have your party catered, give thought to the Ayurvedic balance of the menu, providing all six tastes. Pay attention to detail, balance, and surroundings. Provide *churans* for each dosha in a pretty bowl on the table.

Use cloth napkins whenever possible—they don't require a tree to be sacrificed and they make your guests feel honored. Try to avoid paper plates and disposable plastic utensils.

Surround yourself and your guests with fresh flowers. If you don't want to spend money on flowers, go into nature and respectfully gather wildflowers. Fill bowls with pinecones. Scatter fall leaves on the table. Nature provides—you just have to receive her beautiful gifts.

The most important aspect of entertaining is the love with which you do it. If you surround yourself and your friends with a harmonious environment, a beautiful table, and lovingly prepared food, your party will be a success.

Read more about entertaining in chapter 8, Orchestrating a Feast (page 202).

Chapter

2

HOW TO EAT

Of course, you know how to eat. You've been swallowing things in your mouth even before you hatched as a larva all those years ago. If you could see yourself as a budding human in the womb you'd notice that when you're happy and content, you're swallowing. But if Mom is stressed, you feel anxious, your heart speeds up, and your swallowing stops.

Upon our arrival on this planet, we quickly associate the taste of sweet, warm nourishment with the comfort of being close to the woman we love. Ah, the joy and comfort of food in the mouth and food in the belly! At this stage, if we're hungry, we roar loudly a few times and are promptly rewarded with milk on tap.

WHAT WENT WRONG?

As we advance in our independence and begin to suspect that there may actually be someone else out there, we notice that sometimes our hunger needs are not instantly gratified and sometimes the spoon keeps coming at us even when we don't want any more. It's at this point that we may begin to forget what it means to self-refer. By self-referral, we mean the ability to rely upon our own internal signals of comfort and discomfort to regulate our lives. When our tummies are full but the food continues to arrive, we learn not to pay attention to the messages coming from our inner space.

A few years later, when we are able to manipulate the spoon ourselves, we get other messages from our well-intentioned caregivers. These fall into two main sound bites:

Message #1: "Finish everything on your plate . . . there are children starving in _____!"

If you were raised in the United States, it was usually the poor kids in India who were somehow the beneficiaries of you cleaning your plate. Deepak tells us that in his home in New Delhi, he was told that it was the children in China that were going hungry. We suspect that Chinese moms are telling their offspring that they had better finish all their potstickers because there are children in Chicago missing meals.

Message #2: "It's time to eat. Do you think I am running a restaurant?"

As parents, we understand the desire to cook for everyone in the family at the same time and not be at the beck and call of every hungry mouth in the house. However, we all have our own natural rhythms, which may not be completely in sync with everyone else in the household. Although we've all learned from an early age that "breakfast is the most important meal of the day," for some of us this means eating a four-course feast at

7:00 A.M. and for others it means a croissant and a cup of tea at 10:00 A.M.

We are taught at a very early age not to honor the supreme genius of our bodies. We eat when we are not really hungry "because it's time to eat." We don't eat when our bodies are calling for fuel because we are too busy, trying to lose weight, or waiting for "the restaurant to open." We lose the intimate and delicate connection with our inner wisdom as children and spend the rest of our lives trying to regain it.

The workplace of today is designed for productivity. When we all earned our daily bread by farming the land to grow the wheat to bake in it, it was natural for us to feast on our main meal around noon, relax for an hour or so afterward, and then finish our chores. Today we wolf down a sandwich while talking on the phone over lunch, arrive home in the evening tired and hungry, eat a big meal, and go to bed with a full stomach. It's no wonder that so many of us sleep poorly and that functional digestive disorders afflict more than 30 percent of our population.

BACK TO BASICS

It's not that we don't know how to eat; it's just that we've accepted a few confusing messages that get in the way between our bodies and our minds. This is where the ancient system of health from India known as *Ayurveda* comes to the rescue. Ayurveda is a Sanskrit word that translates as the "science of life." Ancient healing systems were not afraid to look at the core issues of being alive, and eating is one of those key components. Basically Ayurveda tells us that the nourishment we get from eating is a result of both the food we take in and our ability to digest it properly. We can have a very healthy diet but if our digestive power is weak, we will not take full advantage of the available nutrition. So how we eat is as important as what we eat. There is an old Ayurvedic expression that says: "If your digestive power is strong, you can convert poison into nectar, but if your digestive power is weak, you can convert nectar into poison."

BODY INTELLIGENCE TECHNIQUES (BITS)

These twelve points are the way to insure that we make the best use of everything that we put into our mouth. We call them Body Intelligence Techniques because they rely on the natural wisdom of the body, which we all have available to us. We've just forgotten them for a while, but being reminded is all it takes to make them lively again in our awareness. Let's review them one by one.

1. Eat in a settled atmosphere. We digest the environment through all five of our senses. If we watch a violent TV show while eating dinner, we metabolize all those stress and fear chemicals our bodies produce at the same time we're consuming our chow mein. We've found that Chinese food doesn't mix well with anxious spices. Better to eat in a quiet, relaxed place with people we love. Joy, comfort, and delight are the best seasonings to go with a delicious meal.

2. Never eat when upset. Although eating an entire cheesecake by ourselves may seem consoling after a fight with our significant other, we recommend waiting a little while before trying to bury emotional pain with a whopping dose of carbohydrate, protein, or fat. Using food to feed an emotional need unfortunately (1) doesn't work and (2) gets stored as toxicity. Process emotional upsets openly and honestly, then celebrate your good work by preparing and enjoying a scrumptious feast with a good friend.

3. Always sit down to eat. We know we're beginning to sound like your grandmother. Sitting down allows you to put your attention on the delectables on your plate. Attention is what activates everything in this universe. Focusing on your food makes it more nourishing.

4. Eat only when hungry. Your appetite is your best friend—listen to it. Think of your hunger as a fuel gauge. Zero is so empty that you are literally starving. Very few Americans have had this experience. Ten is so full you can barely move. Most of us have felt like this at least once after a Thanksgiving meal. We recommend waiting until your appetite is at a 2 or 3 before eating. This means you are really hungry but will survive if you have to wait an hour. Then once you *sit* to eat, go until you are at a 7—then stop. Seven is the point where you are comfortably full. You could eat more but your hunger is satiated.

5. Reduce ice-cold food and drink. Your taste buds and digestive juices work best at body temperature. The things we tend to take ice cold (beer, sodas) usually don't taste that good at body temperature so we try to sneak them past our taste buds by first numbing them with ice. Of course, ice cream doesn't do well at 98.6 degrees, so we recommend eating this treat at midday when our digestive power is strongest.

6. Don't talk while chewing your food. Attention is empowering. Hear, feel, see, taste, and smell each morsel as it enters you. This allows your system to get the greatest nourishment per chew.

7. Eat at a moderate pace. If you pace yourself throughout the meal and remain in present moment awareness, you will never overeat. It's when we're doing other things while eating (watching TV, talking on the phone, balancing the checkbook) that we lose contact with our inner signals. If we are moving really fast, we will probably zoom past level 7 on the appetite gauge and then wonder why we ate that last helping.

8. Eat freshly cooked meals. The Sanskrit word *prana* means "life force." The more *prana* we take in, the more vital energy we have available to us. Locally grown, freshly prepared foods carry the highest value of life force. Ideally, the farmer, the grocery store clerk, and the cook are all happy, loving people so their nourishing life force contributes to the *prana* of the meal.

9. Reduce raw foods. We know that many diets over the years have strongly encouraged the use of raw foods. There is no doubt that overcooking destroys vitamins and other essential nutrients. Properly cooked foods

(1) taste and smell much better and (2) are easier to digest. We invented fire a while ago because, in addition to keeping us warm and scaring away saber-toothed cats, it made it easier to digest our meals.

10. Experience all six tastes at every meal: *sweet, sour, salty, pungent, bitter, and astringent.* These are the six tastes that make the culinary world go round. If all six are represented at each meal, it will be nutritionally balanced and you will feel satisfied after eating it.

11. Leave one-third to one-quarter of your stomach empty. Leaving some space in the stomach makes digestion a lot easier. Pay attention to level 7 on your appetite gauge and you'll have enough room in your belly to digest the scrumptious nourishing fuel.

12. Sit quietly for a few minutes after your meal. Let your attention be in your body for a little while after you eat. A miracle is in process. Packages of energy and information that were outside of you just moments ago are being transformed in your body. Eating is a magical, spiritual experience. Savor it for a few moments.

FLUNC FOOD (FROZEN, LEFTOVER, UNNATURAL, NUKED, CANNED)

Don't strain. Food is for nourishment. Although we can create a lot of drama around eating, we think it should be easy and joyful. Our recommendation is to use fresh and freshly prepared food *whenever possible.* According to Ayurveda, food provides more than carbohydrates, proteins, fats, vitamins, minerals, and trace elements. It also carries intelligence—life force, *prana*—and the fresher the food the more life force is available. Therefore frozen or canned string beans are not as rich in *prana*, even if they have the same grams of carbohydrates, as beans picked fresh from your garden. However, if you cannot always find the ideal fresh source, don't fret. How you eat is as important as what you eat. If while you are preparing and eating your meal there is joy and love in your heart, the *prana* will be there.

Whenever possible we recommend traditional heat sources for cooking. Microwave ovens were hard to come by five thousand years ago when the ancient Ayurvedic texts were written so they don't have a lot to say about them. Our main contention with microwaves is that they are usually resorted to when we are in a big hurry to heat up frozen or leftover foods, neither of which are terribly rich in *prana*. If you find yourself "nuking" a lot, it's probably a sign that your life is moving too fast and there's some static in your mind-body connection that needs attention.

VEGETARIANISM

If you eat your vegetables, you'll live longer and be healthier and kinder to your wallet and to the earth. A vegetarian diet can be creative, delicious, and balanced and provide plenty of protein, vitamins, and minerals. Both heart disease and cancer, the two biggest killers in our society, are much less likely in people who don't eat animals. From an ecological perspective, a pound of hamburger requires about sixteen pounds of grain, making the eating of meat costly in terms of global food resources. Finally, there is the issue of karma, in which the taking of life and its attendant fear and suffering has its repercussions.

On the other hand, many of our evolutionary ancestors were hunters and we have the biological ability to eat just about anything—animal or vegetable. Our recommendation on this issue is to eat with awareness. Whatever you are allowing into your mind or body, do so consciously and with honor and respect, giving thanks to the source of the nourishment.

Because we are primarily vegetarians ourselves, the recipes in *A Simple Celebration* are meatless. For any of the recipes that call for eggs, you can use egg substitutes or replacers. Remember, though, be sure to follow the directions on the egg substitute or replacer packages accordingly when using. Here again, our watchwords are: *Don't strain*. If Aunt Sophie invited us for dinner and served a savory chicken soup that she had been lovingly preparing all day, we would joyfully eat it because the love in her cooking would provide incomparable nourishment.

FOOD FETISHES

Over the years, many foods have been targeted as the source of a host of health problems. The common problem foods that we hear about at The Chopra Center for Well Being are dairy products, wheat, sugar, sweet fruits, nightshade vegetables, foods with yeast, refined foods, cooked foods, and raw foods. We recognize that people can have sensitivities and intolerances for many common food items and that restricting their intake can relieve symptoms.

We think it's important, however, to remember that how we digest what we eat is as important as what we eat. According to Ayurveda, if our digestive power is strong and balanced, we can eat almost anything and get the nourishment we need. If our digestion is weak, even simple foods can cause problems. If certain common foods seem to be creating problems, look into what might be creating the digestive weakness. The need to have dietary restrictions will often vanish when we strengthen our digestive power. Follow the Body Intelligence Techniques (BITS) (page 18) and the whole environment will be seen as a source of nourishment.

Chapter

3

ANCIENT WISDOM, MODERN NEED

Here we are approaching the millennium where we are breaking the genetic code, surfing cyberspace, and building space stations to explore the galaxies. What value is there in referring *back* to ancient knowledge from thousands of years ago? It's a good question. Our answer is that the great seers of the past were explorers of *inner* space and brought back a wealth of precious insights that are as valuable today as they were in bygone times. They delved into the field of consciousness, which modern science is now acknowledging as being more fundamental to life than atoms and molecules. We can use this knowledge to help create health and happiness and we are delighted to share this information with you so all aspects of your life can be nourishing.

At The Chopra Center for Well Being we help people enliven their inner healer. To accomplish this, we place a lot of attention on food and nutrition because learning to nourish ourselves is the basis of health and happiness. There are few joys in life greater than enjoying a delicious meal with people we love. This joy is transformed in our bodies into rejuvenating and healing chemical messengers that course through our vessels, communicating this love of life to every cell in our body.

In both the Eastern and Western traditions, food is basic to life and to health. In the Vedas, the ancient wisdom tradition of India, there is the saying "Food is Brahman (pure potentiality), Brahman is food." Hippocrates, the father of modern medicine, said, "Let food be your medicine and medicine be your food."

Ayurveda, the ancient system of health from India, is the basis of our programs. Although Ayurveda was first understood in India, its principles are universal and easily translate to our modern Western lifestyle. We don't have to eat Indian food every day to benefit from this wonderful body of knowledge.

According to Ayurveda, each of us inherits a proportion of three basic mind-body principles, called doshas, which create our unique mental and physical characteristics. Most of us have one or two doshas that are most lively in our nature, with the remaining one(s) less significant. The three doshas are known as **Vata, Pitta,** and **Kapha.**

If we have mostly **Vata** dosha, we tend to be thin, light, and quick in our thoughts and actions. Change is a constant part of our lives. When **Vata** is balanced, we are creative, enthusiastic, and lively. But if **Vata** becomes excessive, we may develop anxiety, insomnia, or irregular digestion.

If **Pitta** dosha is most lively in our nature, we tend to be muscular, smart, and determined. If **Pitta** is balanced, we are warm, intelligent, and a good leader. If out of balance, **Pitta** can make us critical, irritable, and aggressive.

If we have mostly **Kapha** dosha in our nature, we tend to have a heavier frame, think and move more leisurely, and are stable. When balanced, **Kapha** creates calmness, sweetness, and loyalty. When excessive, **Kapha** can cause us to gain weight, be congested, and resist healthy change.

Using the principles of Ayurveda, we can identify our mind-body nature and use this understanding to make the most nourishing choices.

Take a few minutes to complete the questionnaire below, rating each statement as to how well it applied to you over the past year.

	not at all	slightly	somewhat	moderately	very
• I tend to think and act quickly.	1	2	3	(4)	5
• I am lively and enthusiastic by nature.	1	2	3	(4)	5
• I tend to be thin and rarely gain weight.	1	(2)	3	4	5
• My daily schedule of eating meals, going to sleep, and awakening tends to vary from day to day.	1	(2)	3	4	5
• Under stress, I tend to worry and become anxious.	1	2	(3)	4	5
• I speak quickly and am a lively conversationalist.	1	2	3	(4)	5
• My feet and hands tend to be cool.	1	(2)	3	4	5
• I tend to have difficulty falling asleep and awaken easily.	1	2	3	(4)	5
• My digestion tends to be irregular, with frequent gas or bloating.	1	2	(3)	4	5
• I tend to eat quickly, finishing my meals before others at my table.	1	(2)	3	4	5

Total for this section (v) __30__

	not at all	slightly	somewhat	moderately	very
• My skin is sensitive, sunburns, or breaks out easily.	1	2	3	4	(5)
• I have a tendency toward indigestion or heartburn.	1	2	(3)	4	5
• I tend to be a perfectionist with a low tolerance for errors.	1	2	3	(4)	5

- It is not uncommon for me to have more than one bowel movement per day.   1   2   ③   4   5

- I feel rested with less than eight hours of sleep.   1   2   3   ④   5

- I think critically, am a good debater, and can argue a point forcefully.   1   2   3   4   ⑤

- When pressured, I tend to become irritable and impatient.   1   2   3   4   ⑤

- If I begin a new project, I tend not to stop until I've completed it.   1   2   ③   4   5

- I have a strong appetite and can eat large quantities of food if I choose.   1   2   3   4   ⑤

- I tend to perform my activities with precision and orderliness.   1   2   3   ④   5

Total for this section (P) ___41___

- I am a good listener. I tend to speak only when I feel that I have something important to say.   1   2   ③   4   5

- I have a tendency to have chronic sinus congestion, asthma, or excessive phlegm.   1   2   ③   4   5

- I have a slow digestion and tend to feel heavy after eating.   1   ②   3   4   5

- I tend to eat slowly.   1   2   3   ④   5

- My skin is usually soft and smooth.   1   2   ③   4   5

- I tend to perform activities in a slow-paced manner.   ①   2   3   4   5

- I tend to be loyal and devoted in my relationships.   1   2   ③   4   5

- I tend to gain weight easily and
  have difficulty losing extra pounds. (1)   2   3   4   5
- I tend to be steady and methodical,
  with consistent energy and endurance. (1)   2   3   4   5
- I tend to be calm by nature and
  seldom lose my temper.   (1)   2   3   4   5

Total for this section (K) _____22_____

V_____30_____   P_____41_____   K_____22_____

Now add up the scores for each of the three sections that correspond to **Vata, Pitta,** and **Kapha.** Rank the three doshas from highest to lowest in your nature. The dosha that scores the highest is usually the one that needs to be balanced.

Every wisp of experience that we have influences the balance of doshas in our mind-body constitution. If we listen to fast-paced, rock and roll music, it will increase **Vata** and decrease **Kapha.** A sweet Brahms lullaby will have the opposite effect. For each of the five senses, every experience can be classified by how it affects each of the doshas.

CREATING BALANCE THROUGH THE SENSES

SENSE OF SMELL

	BALANCES THE DOSHA
VATA	Floral, fruity, warm, sweet, sour aromas— *basil, bergamot, patchouli, vanilla*
PITTA	Cool and sweet aromas— *sandalwood, mint, rose, jasmine*
KAPHA	Stimulating, spicy, aromatic aromas— *eucalyptus, musk, camphor, juniper, clove*

SENSE OF SIGHT

	BALANCES THE DOSHA
VATA	Quiet, peaceful scenery— *blue, gold colors*
PITTA	Cool, soothing scenery *blue, green colors*
KAPHA	Stimulating, lively scenery *red, orange colors*

SENSE OF TOUCH

	BALANCES THE DOSHA
VATA	Gentle, nurturing massage *with sesame or almond oil*
PITTA	Slow, moderate pressure massage *with coconut or olive oil*
KAPHA	Deep stimulating massage *with sesame or mustard oil*

SENSE OF HEARING

	BALANCES THE DOSHA
VATA	Slow-paced, gentle, relaxing rhythms and melodies
PITTA	Medium-paced, sweet, soothing, calming rhythms and melodies
KAPHA	Quick-paced, invigorating, energizing rhythms and melodies

SENSE OF TASTE

When talking about food, the sense of taste is what it's all about. How things taste is how we discovered what was yummy and what was yucky in the first place. Animals and our early human ancestors continuously sampled the surrounding scenery and if it was pleasing to the tongue, it was a pretty safe sign that more could be consumed. If the flavor of the dangling sphere wrapped in its crimson skin was mouthwateringly sweet, we took this as a sign from Mother Nature that the fruit was edible. If the leaf on a bush was intensely bitter, we tended not to add too much of it to our salad for the day.

The word for taste in Ayurveda is *rasa*. It's an interesting word that also means "emotion" and "sap." *Rasa* recognizes that how something tastes in our mouth affects our moods and influences our sense of well-being at subtle levels.

Six tastes are described in Ayurveda:

Sweet   Sour   Salty   Pungent   Bitter   Astringent

We like **sweet** tastes. You don't have to encourage a tot to eat something sugary. But here, sweet is more than just the flavor of sweeteners; it is any food that is mostly carbohydrate, protein, or fat. So sweet includes pastas, breads, nuts, and meat.

Sour taste adds zest to other flavors. We find it most often in citrus fruits and tomatoes, but it is also present in cheeses, salad dressings, and any aged or fermented food.

Salty taste stimulates digestion and makes our mouths water. We use it most in the form of table salt (sodium chloride), but it is also present in soy sauce, tamari, and a variety of vegetable seasoning blends.

Pungent taste is the hot spicy flavor that comes from chilis and peppers. Although in some cultures (Mexican and Indian, for example) it's a big part of every meal, most of us like just a taste of it to wake up our lazy taste buds.

Bitter taste is the flavor of green, leafy vegetables. It is also found in tea, coffee, and real chocolate. We like bitter in smaller quantities and almost always need to blend other flavors in with it. It tends to be depleting and detoxifying. Most medicinal herbs are bitter.

Astringent taste is really more of a sensation on the tongue and in the mouth. Foods that are astringent make you pucker. Beans and lentils are our major source of the astringent taste. Tea also has this quality. We're insuring a good source of vegetable protein in our diet when we include the astringent taste of legumes.

Body Intelligence Technique # 10 says to have all six tastes present at every meal. If each taste is blended into the symphony of flavors, (1) the food will be delicious, (2) you will feel satisfied when you've finished eating, and (3) the meal will be nutritionally balanced and complete.

THE SIX TASTES AND MIND-BODY BALANCE

Like every other sense, taste influences the doshas. Three tastes increase and three tastes decrease each dosha.

MIND-BODY PRINCIPLE	TASTES THAT INCREASE	TASTES THAT DECREASE
VATA	Pungent, Bitter, Astringent	Sweet, Sour, Salty
PITTA	Pungent, Sour, Salty	Sweet, Bitter, Astringent
KAPHA	Sweet, Sour, Salty	Pungent, Bitter, Astringent

Depending upon which mind-body principle is most prominent in your nature, you may wish to favor foods that are balancing (reducing) to that dosha. So if you are a **Vata** type and having a spell where you're feeling more anxious and having trouble sleeping, you might create meals that have more sweet, sour, and salty tastes with less pungent, bitter, and astringent flavors. On the other hand, if **Kapha** is dominating, you would favor the pungent, bitter, and astringent foods (more leafy vegetables and beans) and back off on the sweet flavors (pastas and breads). This doesn't mean to avoid any taste altogether—it just means to shift the balance.

Below is a catalog of which foods to favor or reduce for each mind-body type. We can't overemphasize that this doesn't mean getting compulsive about it! Just have the principles in your awareness and listen to your inner messages. If your list says to increase brussels sprouts and you just hate those little cabbages, then go with your internal signals and find something you like.

Each recipe in this book is categorized according to its influence on the doshas. To emphasize that we are not into straining austerity, the choices for each mind-body type are: less, some, or more. If you are a **Pitta** type and the recipe is *less* for **Pitta,** this means that you should reduce the helping you take of this dish versus another dish that is rated *more* for **Pitta. Some** means use your judgment. If you are cooking for people with a variety of mind-body types, you don't have to prepare three different meals. The mouths you are feeding simply take more of some dishes and less of others. It's really easy and remember, eating is a *celebration!*

VATA-BALANCING DIET

Vata is drying, cooling, and light so favor foods that are oily, warming, and heavy in quality. The best tastes to pacify or balance **Vata** are **sweet, sour,** and **salty.** Take less of foods that are pungent, bitter, and astringent.

RECOMMENDATIONS

1. To balance the lightness of **Vata** eat larger quantities, but do not overeat.

2. Dairy products pacify **Vata.** Boil milk before drinking it and take it warm.

3. All sweeteners pacify **Vata** and may be taken in moderation.

4. Fats and oils reduce **Vata.**

5. Rice and wheat are the best grains. Reduce the amount of barley, corn, millet, buckwheat, rye, and oats.

6. Favor sweet, heavy fruits such as avocados, bananas, berries, cherries, grapes, mangoes, sweet oranges, papayas, peaches, pineapples, and plums. Reduce dry or light fruits like apples, cranberries, pears, and pomegranates.

7. Cooked vegetables are best. Raw vegetables should be minimized. Favor asparagus, beets, and carrots. Other vegetables, such as peas, broccoli, cauliflower, zucchini, and potatoes, may be taken in moderation if well cooked in ghee (clarified butter) or oil. Sprouts and cabbage tend to produce gas and should be minimized.

8. Spices known to pacify **Vata** are cardamom, cumin, ginger, cinnamon, salt, cloves, mustard seed, and black pepper. **Vata** *churans* are also useful.

9. All varieties of nuts are recommended.

10. Except for tofu and mung dahl, reduce the intake of beans.

11. For nonvegetarians, chicken, turkey, and seafood are best; beef should be minimized.

LIGHTER VATA-BALANCING DIET

Although oily, heavier, sweeter, and richer foods are usually recommended to pacify **Vata,** sometimes lighter foods with **Vata**-pacifying qualities are desirable. For example, if you find yourself overeating out of nervousness or anxiety, a *lighter* **Vata** diet will help to settle your mind without adding pounds to your body.

RECOMMENDATIONS

1. Rice, wheat, and oats, prepared with reduced amounts of oil or sweeteners, are the favored grains.

2. All sweeteners may be taken in *reduced* amounts.

3. Favor low-fat milk and lassi. Reduce your quantities of cheese and cream.

4. All oils except for coconut can be used in small quantities. *Small* amounts of ghee may be taken.

5. Green or yellow mung beans and red lentils are preferable. They are usually prepared by mixing one part dried beans with two parts water and boiling to the consistency of soup.

6. Vegetables should be well cooked and are best taken in soups, casseroles, and stews. Almost all vegetables are acceptable, with carrots, zucchini, asparagus, spinach, tomato, and artichoke most desirable.

7. Favor sweet, ripe fruits in season. Figs, pineapples, grapes, apricots, sweet oranges, papayas, and small amounts of raisins are acceptable.

8. The warmer and sweeter spices are useful, including ginger, cumin, cinnamon, cardamom, fennel, cloves, hing (asafoetida), and anise. Salt, lemon juice, and tamarind are also fine in small amounts.

PITTA-BALANCING DIET

Pitta dosha can overheat the mind and body, so favor cool foods and liquids. Foods with **sweet, bitter,** and **astringent** tastes are best. Reduce foods that are pungent, salty, and sour.

RECOMMENDATIONS

1. To balance the heat of **Pitta,** take milk, butter, and ghee. Use less yogurt, cheese, sour cream, and buttermilk, as the sour taste aggravates **Pitta.**

2. All sweeteners, except molasses and honey, may be taken in moderation.

3. Olive, sunflower, and coconut oils are best to pacify **Pitta.** Use less sesame, almond, and corn oil, which are more heating.

4. Wheat, rice, barley, and oats are the best grains to reduce **Pitta.** Use less corn, rye, millet, and brown rice.

5. Sweeter fruits, such as grapes, melons, cherries, coconuts, avocados, mangoes, pomegranates, and fully ripe pineapples, oranges, and plums, are recommended. Reduce sour fruits, such as grapefruits, apricots, and berries.

6. Vegetables to favor are asparagus, cucumbers, potatoes, sweet potatoes, green leafy vegetables, pumpkins, broccoli, cauliflower, celery, okra, lettuce, green beans, and zucchini. Reduce tomatoes, hot peppers, carrots, beets, eggplant, onions, garlic, radishes, and spinach.

7. **Pitta** types need to use seasonings that are more soothing and cooling. These include cinnamon, coriander, cardamom, and fennel. Hotter spices such as ginger, cumin, black pepper, fenugreek, clove, salt, and mustard seed should be used sparingly. Very hot seasonings such as chili peppers and cayenne are best avoided. **Pitta** *churans* are also useful.

8. For nonvegetarians, chicken, pheasant, and turkey are preferable; beef, seafood, and eggs increase **Pitta** and should be minimized.

KAPHA-BALANCING DIET

Kapha dosha is heavy, oily, and cold, so favor foods that are light, dry, and warm. Foods with **pungent, bitter,** and **astringent** tastes are most beneficial for pacifying **Kapha.** Reduce foods with sweet, sour, and salty tastes.

RECOMMENDATIONS

1. Dairy products tend to increase **Kapha** so low-fat milk is best. Boiling milk before drinking it makes it easier to digest. Adding turmeric or ginger to milk before boiling reduces its **Kapha**-increasing qualities.

2. Apples and pears, which are considered lighter fruits, are recommended. Reduce heavier fruits like bananas, avocados, coconuts, melons, dates, figs, or sour oranges.

3. Honey is a sweetener that is said to pacify **Kapha.** Other sweeteners increase **Kapha** and should be reduced.

4. All beans, except for soybeans and tofu, are good for **Kapha** types.

5. Favor the grains of barley, corn, millet, buckwheat, rye, and oats. Reduce the intake of rice and wheat.

6. Reduce all nuts.

7. All spices except salt are pacifying to **Kapha. Kapha** *churans* are also useful.

8. All vegetables except for tomatoes, cucumbers, sweet potatoes, and zucchini are suitable for **Kapha** types.

9. For nonvegetarians, white chicken meat, turkey, and seafood are acceptable. Reduce the intake of red meats.

MAKING IT REALLY EASY — CHURANS OR HERBAL/SPICE BLENDS

The mystery and magic of cooking is in the spicing. Just as every food influences each mind-body principle, so does every herb and spice. Blends of dosha-balancing seasonings are available or can be prepared to be used in cooking or sprinkled on food during a meal. These herb and spice blends (*churans*) insure that each taste is represented in the right proportion. **Vata, Pitta,** and **Kapha** types eating the same pasta primavera can use the appropriate *churan* to personalize their meal.

ABOUT DIETING

Nature expresses her creativity in the variety of shapes and forms that we cherish in the world around us. In our appreciation for the wisdom of nature, we honor the uniqueness of each human being. A daffodil has a different size, shape, and color than an iris and we can appreciate the beauty of both. The idea that we all need to strive for an idealized "perfect" body contrasts with our understanding that nature intentionally and lovingly creates diversity. Nutritional programs that deprive you of food, require strict calorie counting, or recommend prolonged use of synthesized, liquefied substances do not enhance balance and can rarely be sustained. For those of you who wish to shed unwanted pounds, we recommend eating consciously using the Body Intelligence Techniques (BITS) (page 18), following an exercise program appropriate to your mind-body type, and reducing the amount of fat in your diet while following a dosha-balancing regimen.

Many of the recipes in *A Simple Celebration* are naturally low in fat and/or calories and are marked with a heart ♥. Favoring these recipes will help you to realize your weight loss goals while allowing you to fully participate in the celebration of nourishment.

Chapter

4

RECIPES FOR
NUTRITIONAL BLISS

Regardless of your predominant dosha you can enjoy each one of these recipes. Ayurveda is not a system of restriction but rather one that focuses on balance. For each recipe, the main tastes are listed and a recommendation is made regarding the quantity that should be consumed based upon your dosha. For example, if you are a **Kapha** type and a recipe suggests that you take less of that dish, this does not mean you have to avoid it altogether. It simply means that on a relative basis, other dishes that are more pacifying to **Kapha** should be taken in greater quantity. If two doshas are fairly equally represented in your physiology, favor foods that are balancing to both of those doshas. Again, we cannot emphasize enough that eating with awareness insures that the quality and quantity of the food you consume will provide the ideal nourishment for your mind and body.

Appetizers and Snacks

◆

Appetizers should tease the appetite, not fill the tummy. When serving appetizers, remember to bring them to room temperature or slightly warm them (cold food before a meal kills *agni,* or digestive fire). Think of the balance and general tastes of your meal when planning a menu with appetizers.

Snacks are often satisfying enough for an evening meal when balanced and filling. Chutneys enhance the flavors of many snack items, so be sure to look into Condiments and Beverages (page 162) for preparation.

ASIAN EGGS

BABA GHANOUJ

BLACK BEAN DIP

BLUEBERRY BLISS BALLS

BRUSCHETTA

CHILI CHICKPEAS

CURRIED COCONUT ALMONDS

GUACAMOLE AND CHAPPATI CRISPS

HUMMUS DIP

HUMMUS DIP, THAI STYLE

SHAKTI DATE BALLS

RICE AND PEAS SNACK

SAVORY TORTE

ZIPPY ALMONDS

ASIAN EGGS

◆

These delicate eggs are spicy and sweet.

25 minutes to prepare

12 hard-boiled eggs *(sweet)*
1 tablespoon unsalted butter *(sweet)*
2 tablespoons sesame seeds *(sweet)*
½ teaspoon cumin *(pungent)*

⅛ teaspoon garam masala *(pungent)*
⅛ teaspoon turmeric *(bitter, pungent, astringent)*

1. Slice the eggs in half lengthwise.
2. Heat the butter in a skillet. Add the sesame seeds and spices and cook for 30 seconds.
3. Carefully place the eggs, cut sides down, in the skillet. Cook for 2 minutes. Turn the eggs over carefully so they don't come apart. Cook for 2 more minutes.
4. Serve warm or at room temperature.

Serves 6

Prominent Tastes: *Sweet, Pungent*	
If you want to reduce	*eat*
VATA	MORE
PITTA	SOME
KAPHA	LESS

ℬABA 𝒢HANOUJ

◆

Serve this with pita bread or lavash.

45 minutes to prepare

1 large eggplant, peeled and cut into strips *(bitter)*

½ cup sesame tahini *(sweet)*

Juice of 1 lemon *(sour, astringent)*

1 teaspoon Bragg's Liquid Aminos *(astringent, salty)*

1 garlic clove, minced *(all but sour)*

Paprika, to taste *(pungent)*

1 teaspoon olive oil *(sweet)*

1 teaspoon chopped fresh mint or cilantro *(pungent)*

1. Preheat the oven to 350° F.
2. Place the eggplant strips in a baking dish in the oven for approximately 30 minutes, or until soft and tender. Reserve the liquid. Cool the eggplant completely and place in a food processor with all the remaining ingredients, including the reserved liquid. (For very different tastes, choose either mint or cilantro.) Blend well.
3. Refrigerate until 1 hour before serving.

Serves 6 to 8

Prominent Tastes: *Bitter, Pungent, Sweet*	
If you want to reduce	*eat*
VATA	LESS
PITTA	MORE
KAPHA	SOME

♥ℬLACK ℬEAN ᴅIP

◆

*This dip can be made ahead by soaking the beans one day,
cooking the next, and preparing the day of the party. It goes well
with Guacamole and Chappati Crisps (page 46).*

20 minutes to prepare (not including time to cook beans)

1 cup dry black beans *(sweet, astringent)*

1 garlic clove, minced *(all but sour)*

1 teaspoon vegetable broth powder *(all)*

1 teaspoon cumin *(pungent)*

1 teaspoon Bragg's Liquid Aminos *(astringent, salty)*

2 tablespoons minced scallions or 1 tablespoon dry onion flakes *(pungent)*

2 tablespoons minced fresh cilantro *(pungent)*

1. Soak the beans overnight in 3 cups of water. In the morning, drain and rinse the beans well to remove any foam. Place in a pot with 3 more cups of water and bring to a boil. Reduce to a simmer and cook until the beans are quite tender, about 2 hours, adding more water, if necessary. Be sure to skim off any foam that rises to the top while cooking; this reduces the flatulent character of the beans. Cool to room temperature.
2. Mash well and blend with the remaining ingredients. If the dip is too thick, add a little more water to give it a good dipping consistency.
3. Refrigerate until 1 hour before serving.

Serves 6 to 8

Prominent Tastes: *Sweet, Pungent, Astringent*	
If you want to reduce	*eat*
VATA	SOME
PITTA	LESS
KAPHA	SOME

Blueberry Bliss Balls

◆

These little yummies are a favorite energy source for between meals or as a light dessert.

20 minutes to prepare

1 cup dried blueberries *(sweet)*
½ cup pine nuts *(sweet)*
½ cup coconut plus ¼ cup
  coconut, for rolling *(sweet)*

¼ cup sunflower seeds *(sweet, bitter)*
2 teaspoons maple syrup *(sweet)*

1. Place the blueberries and pine nuts in a food processor. Process for about 1 minute. Pour in the ½ cup coconut, sunflower seeds, and maple syrup and process for an additional 20 seconds.
2. Scoop out 1 teaspoon at a time, form into balls, and roll in the remaining ¼ cup coconut. Refrigerate for at least 30 minutes to firm the balls.
3. These can be stored in an airtight container in the refrigerator.

Serves 12

Prominent Taste: *Sweet*	
If you want to reduce	*eat*
VATA	MORE
PITTA	SOME
KAPHA	LESS

♥ ℬRUSCHETTA

❖

Make this in summer with tomatoes right off the vine.

20 minutes to prepare

<u>Bruschetta Topping</u>

1 pound fresh, vine-ripened roma
   tomatoes, chopped and drained
   (sweet, sour)
1 garlic clove, minced *(all but sour)*
1 tablespoon minced scallions
   (pungent, sweet)

1 teaspoon lemon zest *(bitter)*
Juice of 1 lemon *(sour, astringent)*

8 slices of bread or 1 recipe
   Foccacia (page 132) *(sweet)*
¼ cup olive oil, optional *(sweet)*
1 cup minced fresh basil *(pungent)*

1. Blend the bruschetta topping ingredients in a small bowl. Refrigerate until 1 hour before serving.
2. Toast the bread or make the foccacia, brushing with olive oil, if desired, before toasting or baking.
3. Add the fresh basil to the topping mixture just before serving.
4. Serve the warm toast or foccacia with bowls of the bruschetta topping.

Serves 6 to 8

Prominent Tastes: *Sweet, Pungent, Astringent*	
If you want to reduce	eat
VATA	MORE
PITTA	LESS
KAPHA	MORE

♥CHILI CHICKPEAS
◆

Serve this quick, spicy filling with chappatis or pita bread for a snack, lunch, or dinner.

20 minutes to prepare

2 cups cooked chickpeas, drained *(sweet, astringent)*

1 tablespoon Thai-style chili paste *(pungent)*

¼ teaspoon lemongrass *(pungent, sour)*

1 tablespoon Bragg's Liquid Aminos *(astringent, salty)*

¼ cup light coconut milk *(sweet)*

2 tablespoons finely chopped fresh cilantro *(pungent)*

1. Heat a small sauté pan over medium heat. Add the chickpeas, chili paste, lemongrass, and Bragg's Liquid Aminos. Stir frequently. Cook until the chili paste is melted and the chickpeas begin to brown, about 10 minutes.
2. Add the coconut milk and cook an additional 5 minutes, until somewhat thickened. Remove from heat.
3. Toss with the cilantro just before serving.

Serves 4 to 8

Prominent Tastes: *Sweet, Pungent*	
If you want to reduce	*eat*
VATA	SOME
PITTA	LESS
KAPHA	MORE

CURRIED COCONUT ALMONDS

◆

Almonds are sweet and slightly bitter. Soaking them overnight increases their digestibility.

20 minutes to prepare

½ teaspoon ghee or olive oil *(sweet)*

2 cups whole almonds, soaked overnight and dried *(sweet, bitter)*

1 garlic clove, minced or crushed *(all but sour)*

1 teaspoon Bragg's Liquid Aminos *(astringent, salty)*

1 teaspoon chili flakes or ½ teaspoon chili paste *(pungent)*

¼ teaspoon turmeric *(pungent)*

¼ teaspoon ground ginger *(pungent, sweet)*

¼ teaspoon cinnamon *(pungent, bitter)*

¼ teaspoon cardamom *(pungent, sweet)*

¼ teaspoon cumin *(pungent)*

1 teaspoon turbinado sugar *(sweet)*

¼ cup dried toasted coconut *(sweet)*

1. In a sauté pan, heat the ghee or oil to the smoking point. Sauté the almonds in the medium-hot ghee or oil for 5 minutes, stirring frequently. Add the garlic, Bragg's Liquid Aminos, chili flakes or paste, spices, and sugar. Toss with the toasted coconut.
2. Turn off the heat. Let stand for 10 minutes, or until completely cooled.
3. These may be stored in an airtight container for weeks.

Serves 8 to 12

Prominent Tastes: *Sweet, Bitter, Pungent*	
If you want to reduce	eat
VATA	MORE
PITTA	SOME
KAPHA	LESS

♥ GUACAMOLE AND CHAPPATI CRISPS

◆

This traditional Mexican dish is low in fat because the chips are baked, not fried.

25 minutes to prepare

Guacamole

3 ripe avocados, mashed *(sweet)*

2 scallions, minced *(pungent, sweet)*

¼ cup minced fresh cilantro *(pungent)*

Juice of 2 limes *(sour)*

1 teaspoon Bragg's Liquid Aminos *(astringent, salty)*

¼ cup plain nonfat yogurt *(sweet, sour)*

Cilantro sprigs *(pungent)*

1 package chappatis or 6 fresh Whole Wheat Chappatis (page 146), cut into strips *(sweet)*

Salt *(salty)*

1. Blend the guacamole ingredients in a small bowl. Garnish with the cilantro sprigs.
2. Brush the chappati strips with warm salted water and place on racks set on baking dishes in a very hot (500° F.) oven for about 10 minutes, or until lightly browned.
3. Serve with the guacamole.

Serves 8 to 12

Prominent Tastes: *Sweet, Pungent, Sour*	
If you want to reduce	*eat*
VATA	MORE
PITTA	SOME
KAPHA	LESS

❤ℋummus 𝒟ip

❖

Our version of Middle Eastern hummus has no added oil, saving oodles of calories. Serve this with pita bread or lavash.

20 minutes to prepare

3 cups cooked chickpeas *(sweet, astringent)*

¼ cup sesame tahini *(sweet)*

Juice of 1 lemon *(sour, astringent)*

¼ to ½ cup orange juice (organic orange juice concentrate may be used for a more intense flavor) *(sweet, sour)*

1 teaspoon Bragg's Liquid Aminos *(astringent, salty)*

1 garlic clove, minced *(all but sour)*

Paprika, to taste *(pungent)*

1 teaspoon chopped fresh cilantro *(pungent)*

1. Place the chickpeas in a food processor and process for 3 minutes, until smooth. Water may be added if the paste becomes too thick to mix. Add the remaining ingredients and process until smooth.
2. Refrigerate until 1 hour before serving.

Serves 8 to 12

Prominent Tastes: *Sweet, Astringent*	
If you want to reduce	eat
VATA	SOME
PITTA	SOME
KAPHA	SOME

♥Hummus Dip, Thai Style

◆

A touch of Thai chili paste adds a new dimension to hummus.
Serve this with pita bread or lavash.

20 minutes to prepare

3 cups cooked chickpeas *(sweet, astringent)*

¼ cup light coconut milk *(sweet)*

Juice of 1 lemon *(sour, astringent)*

¼ to ½ cup orange juice (organic orange juice concentrate may be used for more intense flavor) *(sweet, sour)*

1 teaspoon Bragg's Liquid Aminos *(astringent, salty)*

1 garlic clove, minced *(all but sour)*

1 to 2 teaspoons Thai chili paste *(pungent)*

1 teaspoon chopped fresh cilantro *(pungent)*

1. Place the chickpeas in a food processor and process for 3 minutes, until smooth. Water may be added if the paste becomes too thick to mix. Add the remaining ingredients and process until smooth.
2. Refrigerate until 1 hour before serving.

Serves 8 to 12

Prominent Tastes: *Sweet, Pungent, Astringent*	
If you want to reduce	*eat*
VATA	SOME
PITTA	SOME
KAPHA	SOME

Shakti Date Balls

◆

Here's another high energy snack.

10 minutes to prepare

1 cup dried date pieces *(sweet)*

½ cup walnuts *(sweet)*

½ cup coconut *(sweet)*

¼ cup sunflower seeds *(sweet, bitter)*

2 teaspoons honey *(sweet)*

¼ cup toasted sesame seeds, for rolling *(sweet)*

1. Place the dates, walnuts, coconut, and sunflower seeds in a food processor. Process for about 1 minute, until well chopped but not pulverized. Pour in the honey and process for an additional 20 seconds.
2. Scoop out 1 teaspoon at a time, form into balls, and roll in sesame seeds. Refrigerate for at least 30 minutes to firm the balls.
3. These can be stored in an airtight container in the refrigerator.

Serves 4 to 6

Prominent Taste: *Sweet*	
If you want to reduce	*eat*
VATA	MORE
PITTA	SOME
KAPHA	LESS

❤ RICE AND PEAS SNACK

◆

5 minutes to prepare

1 cup cooked basmati rice *(sweet)*
½ cup cooked fresh or frozen
   organic peas *(sweet, astringent)*
1 tablespoon currants *(sweet)*
1 teaspoon Bragg's Liquid Aminos
   (astringent, salty)

1 teaspoon lemon juice *(sour,
   astringent)*
Dash of grated nutmeg *(pungent,
   astringent)*
1 teaspoon ghee, optional *(sweet)*

Toss all the ingredients together.

Serves 4 to 6

Prominent Taste: *Sweet*	
If you want to reduce	*eat*
VATA	MORE
PITTA	SOME
KAPHA	SOME

SAVORY TORTE

◆

*Here's a quick, delicious appetizer using a quick, frozen specialty.
This is one of those times when frozen is much preferred to
making your own pastry dough, since making your own would
increase the time by about 3 hours! Make sure your other
ingredients are fresh, fresh, fresh.*

45 minutes to prepare

1 package Pepperidge Farm Puff
  Pastry *(sweet)*
4 red onions *(pungent)*
½ teaspoon ghee *(sweet)*
1 yellow pepper *(pungent)*
¼ cup chèvre (goat cheese) *(sweet)*

½ cup chopped sun-dried tomatoes
  (sour)
¼ teaspoon fresh rosemary
  (pungent, bitter)
¼ cup grated Parmesan cheese
  (sweet)

1. Follow the directions on the package of puff pastry for thawing and rolling.
2. In a skillet, sauté the onions in the ghee until well browned and caramelized, about 20 minutes. Set aside to cool.
3. Roast the yellow pepper over a gas flame or electric burner. Cool. Peel the skin away by rubbing between your fingers. Chop the pepper well.
4. Preheat the oven to 400° F.
5. Arrange the pastry on a large oiled cookie sheet or pizza tin, crimping the edges to form a ridge. Spread the chèvre over the surface, then sprinkle all the remaining ingredients over the top, ending with the Parmesan cheese.
6. Bake for 25 minutes, or until the pastry is golden. Serve warm or at room temperature.

Serves 4 to 8

Prominent Tastes: *Sweet, Pungent*	
If you want to reduce	*eat*
VATA	MORE
PITTA	LESS
KAPHA	SOME

Zippy Almonds

◆

Almonds are sweet and slightly bitter. Soaking them overnight increases their digestibility. These almonds have a spicy, fiery flavor—great to boost the appetite.

20 minutes to prepare

½ teaspoon ghee or olive oil *(sweet)*
2 cups whole almonds, soaked overnight and dried *(sweet, bitter)*
1 garlic clove, minced or crushed *(all but sour)*

1 teaspoon Bragg's Liquid Aminos *(astringent, salty)*
1 teaspoon chili flakes or ½ teaspoon chili paste *(pungent)*
1 teaspoon turbinado sugar *(sweet)*

1. Heat the ghee or oil to the smoking point in a skillet. Sauté the almonds in medium-hot ghee or oil for 5 minutes, stirring frequently. Add the garlic, Bragg's Liquid Aminos, chili flakes or paste, and sugar. Toss to coat the almonds.
2. Turn off the heat and let stand for 10 minutes, or until completely cooled.
3. These may be stored in an airtight container for weeks.

Serves 8 to 12

Prominent Tastes: *Sweet, Bitter, Pungent*	
If you want to reduce	*eat*
VATA	MORE
PITTA	LESS
KAPHA	LESS

Soups

◆

Regardless of the season, a great soup is always appreciated. Organic vegetable broth powders are useful to save time, but fresh stocks are always a wonderful contribution to the flavor and nutrition of soup.

ACORN SQUASH SOUP	PUMPKIN SOUP
CURRIED CARROT SOUP	RED LENTIL DAHL
GREEN SPLIT PEA DAHL	SPINACH SOUP
MUNG BEAN KITCHARI	WATERMELON SOUP
POTATO-LEEK SOUP	*(with Beets and Orange)*

♥Acorn Squash Soup

◆

This soup is creamy without cream.

1½ hours to prepare

6 medium acorn squash, cut into
quarters *(sweet)*

4 to 5 cups vegetable stock *(all)*

3 tablespoons vegetable broth
powder *(all)*

2 tablespoons Bragg's Liquid
Aminos *(astringent, salty)*

¼ teaspoon sea salt *(salty)*

1 tablespoon cinnamon *(pungent, bitter)*

½ teaspoon cloves *(pungent)*

½ teaspoon ground ginger
(pungent, sweet)

Plain nonfat yogurt *(sweet, sour)*

1. Place the squash, cut side down, on an oiled or sprayed baking sheet, cover with foil, and bake 45 minutes in a 375°F. oven. Cool.

2. Scoop the pulp from the squash and combine with the vegetable stock, vegetable broth powder, Bragg's Liquid Aminos, salt, cinnamon, cloves, and ginger in a soup pot. Simmer for about 20 minutes. With a hand-held soup blender, mash the pulp to blend well with the stock.

3. Add a scoop of yogurt before serving warm or slightly chilled.

Serves 4 to 6

Prominent Tastes: *Sweet, Pungent*	
If you want to reduce	*eat*
VATA	MORE
PITTA	SOME
KAPHA	SOME

♥CURRIED CARROT SOUP

◆

A light touch of curry gives this carrot soup a tangy zip.

30 minutes to prepare

½ teaspoon olive oil or ghee *(sweet)*

8 medium carrots, cut into pieces *(sweet, pungent)*

½ yellow onion, diced *(pungent, sweet)*

2 tablespoons vegetable broth powder *(all)*

2 tablespoons Bragg's Liquid Aminos *(astringent, salty)*

¼ teaspoon sea salt *(salty)*

1 teaspoon cinnamon *(pungent, bitter)*

½ teaspoon turmeric *(bitter, pungent, astringent)*

½ teaspoon cardamom *(pungent, sweet)*

¼ teaspoon chili flakes *(pungent)*

½ teaspoon ground cloves *(pungent)*

½ teaspoon ground ginger *(pungent, sweet)*

1. Heat the oil or ghee in a stockpot to the smoking point. Sauté the carrots and onion in the oil or ghee for 5 minutes, stirring frequently. Cover with 4 cups of water, bring to a boil, and cook 20 minutes.
2. Add the remaining ingredients. With a hand-held soup blender, process until smooth.
3. Simmer for 10 minutes. Serve warm.

Serves 4 to 6

Prominent Tastes: *Sweet, Pungent*	
If you want to reduce	*eat*
VATA	MORE
PITTA	SOME
KAPHA	MORE

❤Green Split Pea Dahl

◆

Split peas are a reminder of Mom, home, and hearth.

2¹/₂ hours to prepare (not including time to soak beans)

1 cup dried green split peas *(sweet, astringent)*

Pinch of sea salt *(salty)*

1 cup diced carrots *(sweet, pungent)*

1 celery stalk, diced *(bitter, astringent)*

3 tablespoons vegetable broth powder *(all)*

1 teaspoon ghee *(sweet)*

1 tablespoon mustard seeds *(pungent)*

1 teaspoon coriander *(pungent, bitter)*

1 teaspoon turmeric *(bitter, pungent, astringent)*

1-inch piece of fresh gingerroot, grated, or 1 teaspoon ground ginger *(pungent, sweet)*

1 teaspoon cumin *(pungent)*

2 tablespoons Bragg's Liquid Aminos *(astringent, salty)*

1. In a soup pot, soak the peas in 4 cups of water overnight. Drain and rinse well. Add 4 more cups of water, the salt, carrots, celery, and vegetable broth powder. Simmer over low heat for about 2 hours, until tender.

2. In a skillet, heat the ghee to the smoking point. Add the mustard seeds. When they begin to sputter and pop, add to the peas with the remaining ingredients. Simmer over low heat for about 15 minutes.

Serves 6 to 8

Prominent Tastes: *Pungent, Astringent*	
If you want to reduce	*eat*
VATA	LESS
PITTA	SOME
KAPHA	SOME

❤Mung Bean Kitchari

◆

*Legumes and rice mixed together are a complete protein
and a satisfying meal.*

45 minutes to prepare

1 tablespoon ghee or olive oil *(sweet)*

½ teaspoon cumin seeds *(pungent)*

2 bay leaves *(pungent)*

1 teaspoon coriander *(pungent,
bitter)*

1 teaspoon dried oregano *(pungent)*

½ teaspoon sea salt *(salty)*

1 teaspoon grated ginger *(pungent,
sweet)*

½ teaspoon turmeric *(bitter,
pungent, astringent)*

½ cup basmati rice *(sweet)*

½ cup mung beans *(sweet,
astringent)*

½ cup diced carrots *(sweet, pungent)*

½ cup diced celery *(bitter,
astringent)*

1. Melt the ghee or oil in a soup pot. Add the cumin, bay leaves, coriander, oregano, salt, and ginger and stir until slightly browned.
2. Add the turmeric, rice, mung beans, and 3 cups of water. Cook for about 30 minutes.
3. Add the diced carrots and celery and cook an additional 15 minutes.

Serves 4 to 6

Prominent Tastes: *Sweet, Pungent, Astringent*	
If you want to reduce	*eat*
VATA	MORE
PITTA	MORE
KAPHA	SOME

❤Potato-Leek Soup

❤

This is perfect for lunch, with salad greens and warm bread.

30 minutes to prepare

½ teaspoon olive oil or ghee *(sweet)*

8 medium potatoes, diced *(astringent)*

2 large leeks, diced and then washed well *(pungent, sweet)*

2 tablespoons vegetable broth powder *(all)*

2 tablespoons Bragg's Liquid Aminos *(astringent, salty)*

¼ teaspoon sea salt *(salty)*

1 teaspoon tarragon *(pungent)*

½ teaspoon thyme *(pungent)*

½ teaspoon grated nutmeg *(pungent, astringent)*

1. In a stockpot, heat the oil or ghee to the smoking point. Sauté the potatoes and leeks for 5 minutes, stirring frequently. Cover with 4 cups of water, bring to a boil, and cook 20 minutes.

2. Remove from heat and add the remaining ingredients. Let stand for 20 minutes before serving. Reheat if necessary. Serve warm. This soup can also be served puréed.

Serves 6 to 8

Prominent Tastes: *Sweet, Pungent, Astringent*	
If you want to reduce	*eat*
VATA	SOME
PITTA	SOME
KAPHA	SOME

♥Pumpkin Soup

♦

Here's a smooth fall soup with the aroma of a pumpkin pie.

1½ hours to prepare

6 medium pumpkins, preferably sugar pie, cut into quarters *(sweet)*

4 to 5 cups vegetable stock *(all)*

3 tablespoons vegetable broth powder *(all)*

2 tablespoons Bragg's Liquid Aminos *(astringent, salty)*

¼ teaspoon sea salt *(salty)*

1 tablespoon cinnamon *(pungent, bitter)*

½ teaspoon cloves *(pungent)*

½ teaspoon ground ginger *(pungent, sweet)*

1 can (14 ounces) light coconut milk *(sweet)*

Plain nonfat yogurt *(sweet, sour)*

1. Place the pumpkins on an oiled or sprayed baking sheet, cover with foil, and bake 45 minutes in a 375° F. oven. Cool.

2. Scoop the pulp from the pumpkins. Combine with the remaining ingredients except the yogurt in a soup pot. Simmer for about 20 minutes. With a hand-held soup blender, mash the pulp to blend well with the stock.

3. Add a scoop of yogurt before serving.

Serves 4 to 6

Prominent Tastes: *Sweet, Pungent, Astringent*	
If you want to reduce	*eat*
VATA	MORE
PITTA	SOME
KAPHA	SOME

❥RED LENTIL DAHL

◆

Red lentils turn slightly green when cooked.
They cook more quickly than brown or green lentils.

1¹/₂ hours to prepare

1 cup dried red lentils *(sweet, astringent)*

Pinch of sea salt *(salty)*

1 cup diced carrots *(sweet, pungent)*

1 celery stalk, diced *(bitter, astringent)*

3 tablespoons vegetable broth powder *(all)*

1 teaspoon ghee *(sweet)*

1 tablespoon mustard seeds *(pungent)*

1 teaspoon coriander *(pungent, bitter)*

1 teaspoon turmeric *(bitter, pungent, astringent)*

1-inch piece of fresh gingerroot, grated, or 1 teaspoon ground ginger *(pungent, sweet)*

1 teaspoon cumin *(pungent)*

2 tablespoon Bragg's Liquid Aminos *(astringent, salty)*

1. Rinse the lentils well and put in a soup pot. Add 4 cups of water, the salt, carrots, celery, and vegetable broth powder to the lentils. Simmer over low heat for about 1 hour, until tender.
2. In a skillet, heat the ghee to the smoking point. Add the mustard seeds. When they begin to sputter and pop, add to the lentils with the remaining ingredients. Simmer over low heat for about 15 minutes. Serve warm.

Serves 4 to 6

Prominent Tastes: *Pungent, Astringent*	
If you want to reduce	eat
VATA	SOME
PITTA	SOME
KAPHA	MORE

♥SPINACH SOUP

◆

The touch of sugar in this recipe softens the bitterness of the spinach—even your kids will like it.

25 minutes to prepare

1 tablespoon ghee *(sweet)*

8 bunches spinach, cleaned *(bitter)*

6 celery stalks, cut into bite-size pieces *(bitter, astringent)*

5 tablespoons vegetable broth powder *(all)*

6 tablespoons Bragg's Liquid Aminos *(astringent, salty)*

1 teaspoon turbinado sugar *(sweet)*

1 tablespoon tarragon *(pungent)*

1 tablespoon thyme *(pungent)*

½ teaspoon grated nutmeg plus extra, for sprinkling *(pungent, astringent)*

Plain nonfat yogurt *(sweet, sour)*

1. In a large saucepan, heat the ghee to the smoking point. Sauté the spinach until just tender. Barely cover with water and add everything but the nutmeg and yogurt. Simmer for about 10 minutes.

2. Add ½ teaspoon nutmeg and process in a food processor. Serve warm, with a sprinkling of nutmeg and a scoop of yogurt.

Serves 4 to 6

Prominent Tastes: *Bitter, Astringent, Pungent, Sweet*	
If you want to reduce	*eat*
VATA	LESS
PITTA	MORE
KAPHA	SOME

❤ WATERMELON SOUP

(WITH BEETS AND ORANGE)

◆

This is a low-fat, cooling summer soup.

1 hour to prepare

½ teaspoon ghee *(sweet)*

¼ cup chopped shallots *(pungent, sweet)*

2 pounds beets, scrubbed and chopped *(bitter, sweet)*

3 tablespoons vegetable broth powder *(all)*

2 pounds watermelon, cut up and seeded *(sweet)*

1 quart orange juice *(sweet, sour)*

Pinch of sea salt *(salty)*

Plain nonfat yogurt *(sweet, sour)*

Grated nutmeg *(pungent, astringent)*

Fresh mint sprigs *(pungent)*

1. Heat the ghee to the smoking point in a stockpot. Sauté the shallots until soft. Add the beets, vegetable broth powder, and 1 quart of water. Bring to a boil and simmer until the beets are thoroughly cooked and tender. Add the watermelon.

2. Blend the soup in the pot with a hand-held soup blender or process in a food processor. Add the orange juice and salt and beat with a large wooden spoon until well mixed.

3. Serve at room temperature in soup bowls with a dollop of yogurt, a sprinkling of nutmeg, and a sprig of fresh mint.

Serves 4 to 6

Prominent Tastes: *Bitter, Sweet*	
If you want to reduce	*eat*
VATA	MORE
PITTA	LESS
KAPHA	MORE

SALADS

♦

Salads can add delightful color, texture, and taste to a meal. Use your imagination when putting salads and dressings together.

CHAPPATI CRISP SALAD

CLASSIC CHOPPED SALAD

CURRIED TEMPEH SALAD

LENTIL-RICE SALAD

SPINACH GREENS WITH GORGONZOLA

THREE FRUIT SALAD

VEGETARIAN NIÇOISE

WARM WILD RICE SALAD

♥CHAPPATI CRISP SALAD

◆

45 minutes to prepare

6 Whole Wheat Chappatis (page 146) *(sweet)*

2 cups cooked chickpeas *(sweet, astringent)*

1 cup raw fresh corn kernels *(sweet)*

1 cup fresh or frozen peas (if using frozen peas, choose organic if possible and thaw) *(sweet, astringent)*

¼ cup chopped scallions *(pungent, sweet)*

1 cup shredded carrots *(sweet, pungent)*

½ cup chopped celery *(bitter, astringent)*

½ cup chopped fresh cilantro *(pungent)*

Juice of 3 limes *(sour)*

1 tablespoon honey or turbinado sugar *(sweet)*

1 tablespoon Bragg's Liquid Aminos *(astringent, salty)*

2 cups shredded romaine lettuce *(bitter, astringent)*

1. Preheat the oven to 400°F.
2. Brush the chappatis on both sides with warm salted water. Place 6 small ovenproof bowls upside down on a baking sheet and drape each chappati over a bowl. Place in the hot oven and bake for approximately 20 minutes, or until the chappatis are browned. Remove from the oven and cool.
3. Combine the remaining ingredients except the shredded lettuce. Arrange the lettuce in the shells and spoon the salad filling on top.

Serves 6

Prominent Tastes: *Tridoshic*	
If you want to reduce	*eat*
VATA	SOME
PITTA	SOME
KAPHA	SOME

❤CLASSIC CHOPPED SALAD

❦

This salad can be designed for your dosha by using your favorite vegetables and doshic dressing.

30 minutes to prepare

1 broccoli stalk *(bitter, astringent)*

1 head of cauliflower *(sweet, astringent)*

1 pound asparagus *(sweet, bitter, astringent)*

1 cup green beans *(sweet, astringent)*

1 cup fresh corn kernels *(sweet)*

¼ cup currants *(sweet)*

¼ cup pine nuts *(sweet)*

¼ cup finely chopped red onion *(pungent, sweet)*

1 yellow tomato, chopped and drained *(sweet, sour)*

1 cup grated carrots *(sweet, pungent)*

¼ cup finely chopped fennel *(pungent)*

3 tablespoons **Vata, Pitta,** or **Kapha** dressing of your choice (page 77)

1. Chop the broccoli, cauliflower, asparagus, and beans into bite-size pieces. Lightly steam about 3 minutes. Rinse in cold water and let cool to room temperature.
2. Combine with the remaining ingredients and toss with the dressing.

Serves 4 to 6

Prominent Tastes: *Tridoshic*	
If you want to reduce	*eat*
VATA	SOME
PITTA	SOME
KAPHA	MORE

♥Curried Tempeh Salad

◆

This tastes so much like chicken, you'll fool those meat eaters.

45 minutes to prepare

2 packages soy tempeh *(sweet, astringent)*

3 tablespoons minced fresh cilantro *(pungent)*

3 tablespoons chopped fresh parsley *(pungent, astringent)*

¼ cup chopped almonds *(sweet, bitter)*

¼ cup raisins or currants *(sweet)*

¼ cup chopped celery *(bitter, astringent)*

1 teaspoon turmeric *(bitter, pungent, astringent)*

1 teaspoon garam masala of coriander, cumin, cardamom, and cinnamon *(pungent, bitter, sweet)*

1 tablespoon Bragg's Liquid Aminos *(astringent, salty)*

¼ cup plain nonfat yogurt *(sweet, sour)*

⅛ teaspoon sea salt *(salty)*

Lavash *(sweet)*

Shredded romaine lettuce *(bitter, astringent)*

Fresh parsley or cilantro sprigs *(pungent, astringent)*

1. Steam the tempeh in the top of a double boiler for 20 minutes. Cool and crumble with your fingers. Combine all the ingredients except lavash, lettuce, and parsley or cilantro in a large bowl and toss well.

2. Roll into lavash or make into rounds. Serve on a bed of lettuce and garnish with parsley or cilantro sprigs.

Serves 4 to 6

Prominent Tastes: *Sweet, Astringent, Bitter, Pungent*	
If you want to reduce	*eat*
VATA	MORE
PITTA	MORE
KAPHA	LESS

♥ LENTIL-RICE SALAD

◆

Lentils and rice together create complete protein.
Serve this dish on a warm day with Tomato Chutney (page 172)
and Whole Wheat Chappatis (page 146).

25 minutes to prepare

3 carrots, chopped *(sweet, pungent)*

3 cups cooked brown or green lentils, cooled *(sweet, astringent)*

1 cup cooked basmati rice, cooled *(sweet)*

1 cup chopped celery *(bitter, astringent)*

1 cup cooked fresh or frozen organic peas, cooled *(sweet, astringent)*

2 tablespoons finely chopped scallions *(pungent, sweet)*

¼ cup chopped fresh parsley *(pungent, astringent)*

3 tablespoons **Vata, Pitta,** or **Kapha** dressing of your choice (page 77)

1. Blanch the carrots by immersing in a pot of boiling water for 5 minutes. Remove from the pot and immediately rinse until cooled with cold water to stop the cooking and retain color.
2. Combine all the ingredients in a bowl and gently toss with the dressing.

Serves 4 to 6

Prominent Tastes: *Tridoshic*	
If you want to reduce	*eat*
VATA	SOME
PITTA	MORE
KAPHA	MORE

Spinach Greens with Gorgonzola

◆

This is a quick, delicious salad.

20 minutes to prepare

2 pounds washed and stemmed
spinach *(bitter)*
1 cup Honey-Glazed Walnuts,
recipe follows *(sweet)*
½ cup crumbled Gorgonzola cheese
(sweet)

½ cup currants *(sweet)*
3 tablespoons Poppy Seed Dressing
(page 80)

Toss all ingredients together and arrange on plates.

HONEY-GLAZED WALNUTS

½ teaspoon ghee *(sweet)*
1 cup walnut pieces *(sweet)*

1 tablespoon honey *(sweet)*

1. Heat the ghee to the smoking point in a skillet. Toss in the walnuts and sauté 2 minutes, until golden.
2. Add the honey and coat the walnuts well. Let cool completely before using.

Serves 4 to 6

Prominent Tastes: *Bitter, Sweet*	
If you want to reduce	*eat*
VATA	MORE
PITTA	MORE
KAPHA	SOME

Three Fruit Salad

◆

Tomatoes a fruit? Yes. Avocados a fruit? Yes. This salad is more like a chutney and goes well with spicy main dishes. If you can't find yellow tomatoes, red ones will do just as well. Make this in summer, though, when tomatoes are vine ripened and flavorful.

10 minutes to prepare

1 large firm but ripe yellow tomato, diced and drained *(sweet, sour)*

1 firm avocado, diced *(sweet)*

2 firm but ripe nectarines, diced (do not remove skin) *(sweet)*

⅛ teaspoon balsamic vinegar *(sour)*

1 teaspoon dried onion flakes *(pungent, sweet)*

1 teaspoon honey, optional *(sweet)*

1 teaspoon olive oil *(sweet)*

1 teaspoon orange juice *(sweet, sour)*

1 tablespoon Bragg's Liquid Aminos *(astringent, salty)*

4 to 6 romaine lettuce leaves *(bitter, astringent)*

Combine all the ingredients except lettuce in a bowl and toss gently. Serve on lettuce leaves.

Serves 4 to 6

Prominent Tastes: *Sweet, Pungent*	
If you want to reduce	*eat*
VATA	MORE
PITTA	LESS
KAPHA	LESS

69

Vegetarian Niçoise

◆

Although this is traditionally served with tuna,
you'll never miss it.

30 minutes to prepare

2 heads of romaine lettuce, washed, dried, and shredded *(bitter, astringent)*

6 roma tomatoes, cut into bite-size pieces and drained *(sweet, sour)*

½ sweet red onion, finely chopped *(pungent, sweet)*

1 cucumber, peeled, seeded, and chopped *(sweet, astringent)*

1 small jicama, peeled and chopped *(sweet)*

¼ cup finely chopped fresh parsley *(pungent)*

1 small jar capers, drained, juice reserved *(astringent, salty)*

¼ to ½ cup crumbled feta cheese *(sweet)*

⅛ cup olive oil *(sweet)*

⅛ cup orange juice *(sweet, sour)*

1 tablespoon Bragg's Liquid Aminos *(astringent, salty)*

1 teaspoon balsamic vinegar *(sour)*

1 teaspoon honey, optional *(sweet)*

1. Arrange the lettuce on a large platter. Carefully layer the tomatoes, onion, cucumber, jicama, parsley, and capers in an attractive pattern over the lettuce.
2. Combine the remaining ingredients, including the reserved caper juice, in a jar, shake well, and pour over the salad.

Serves 4 to 8

Prominent Tastes: *Sweet, Astringent, Sour*	
If you want to reduce	*eat*
VATA	SOME
PITTA	SOME
KAPHA	SOME

$\mathcal{W}$ARM $\mathcal{W}$ILD $\mathcal{R}$ICE $\mathcal{S}$ALAD

◆

In this different combination the sweetness is balanced by the fennel and fresh herbs.

45 minutes to prepare

3 cups cooked wild and brown rice mix, cooled *(sweet)*

2 avocados, cut into bite-size pieces *(sweet)*

1 cup diced fresh fennel bulb or 2 tablespoons fennel seeds *(pungent)*

1 cup diced celery *(bitter, astringent)*

½ package dried blueberries *(sweet, astringent)*

¼ cup sunflower seeds *(sweet, bitter)*

¼ cup raisins *(sweet)*

¼ cup chopped fresh dill *(pungent)*

¼ cup chopped fresh chives *(pungent)*

Lemon-Lime Dressing, to taste (page 84)

Combine all the ingredients in a bowl and serve at room temperature.

Serves 6 to 8

Prominent Tastes: *Sweet, Pungent*	
If you want to reduce	*eat*
VATA	MORE
PITTA	MORE
KAPHA	LESS

$\mathcal{R}$AITAS

◆

$\mathbf{R}$aitas are salads made with yogurt. They are traditionally served as cooling side dishes to accompany spicy meals.

| CHICKPEA RAITA | PEAR-DATE RAITA |
| CUCUMBER RAITA | POTATO RAITA |

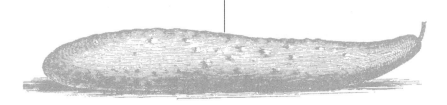

♥CHICKPEA RAITA

◆

25 minutes to prepare

1 teaspoon mustard oil or ghee *(pungent or sweet)*

1 teaspoon black mustard seeds *(pungent)*

1 teaspoon cumin seeds *(pungent)*

2 cups cooked chickpeas *(sweet, astringent)*

1 large cucumber, cut into bite-size pieces *(sweet, astringent)*

¼ cup currants *(sweet)*

1 teaspoon chili flakes *(pungent)*

3 tablespoons finely chopped scallions *(pungent, sweet)*

1 tablespoon finely chopped fresh cilantro *(pungent)*

2 tablespoons Bragg's Liquid Aminos *(astringent, salty)*

1 cup plain nonfat yogurt *(sweet, sour)*

Juice of 1 lemon *(sour, astringent)*

1. Heat the oil or ghee in a small skillet. Toss in the mustard and cumin seeds. When they sputter and pop, remove from the heat. Cool completely.
2. Toss gently with the remaining ingredients. Refrigerate until 1 hour before serving.

Serves 4 to 6

Prominent Tastes: *Pungent, Sweet, Sour*	
If you want to reduce	*eat*
VATA	SOME
PITTA	LESS
KAPHA	LESS

♥Cucumber Raita

◆

25 minutes to prepare

2 medium cucumbers, peeled, seeded, and diced *(sweet, astringent)*

½ cup plain nonfat yogurt *(sweet, sour)*

1 tablespoon minced scallions *(pungent, sweet)*

1-inch piece of fresh gingerroot, grated, or ½ teaspoon ground ginger *(pungent, sweet)*

2 tablespoons finely chopped fresh cilantro *(pungent)*

Juice of 1 lemon *(sour, astringent)*

1 teaspoon honey *(sweet)*

⅛ teaspoon lemon zest *(bitter)*

⅛ teaspoon turmeric *(bitter, pungent, astringent)*

⅛ teaspoon cinnamon *(pungent, bitter)*

⅛ teaspoon cardamom *(pungent, sweet)*

2 tablespoons Bragg's Liquid Aminos *(astringent, salty)*

Combine all the ingredients in a mixing bowl and toss gently. Refrigerate until 1 hour before serving.

Serves 4 to 6

Prominent Tastes: *Tridoshic*	
If you want to reduce	*eat*
VATA	SOME
PITTA	SOME
KAPHA	SOME

$\mathcal{P}$EAR-$\mathcal{D}$ATE $\mathcal{R}$AITA

❖

Replace the pears with apples for a Waldorf salad.

20 minutes to prepare

10 Anjou or Bartlett pears, chopped *(sweet)*

1 cup chopped dates *(sweet)*

½ cup raisins *(sweet)*

½ cup chopped celery *(bitter, astringent)*

½ cup toasted pine nuts *(sweet)*

Juice of 2 lemons *(sour, astringent)*

½ cup plain nonfat yogurt *(sweet, sour)*

¼ cup honey *(sweet)*

Toss all the ingredients together in a bowl. Refrigerate until 1 hour before serving.

Serves 6 to 8

Prominent Tastes: *Astringent, Sweet*	
If you want to reduce	*eat*
VATA	MORE
PITTA	SOME
KAPHA	LESS

❤Potato Raita

◆

40 minutes to prepare

1 teaspoon mustard oil or ghee
   (pungent or sweet)
1 teaspoon black mustard seeds
   (pungent)
1 teaspoon cumin seeds *(pungent)*
3 medium potatoes, preferably
   Yukon Gold or red, scrubbed and
   cut into bite-size pieces *(astringent)*
1 teaspoon chili flakes *(pungent)*

3 tablespoons finely chopped
   scallions *(pungent, sweet)*
1 tablespoon finely chopped fresh
   cilantro *(pungent)*
2 tablespoons Bragg's Liquid
   Aminos *(astringent, salty)*
1 cup plain nonfat yogurt *(sweet,
   sour)*
Juice of 1 lemon *(sour, astringent)*

1. Heat the oil or ghee in a small skillet. Toss in the mustard and cumin seeds. When they sputter and pop, add the potatoes and chili flakes. Sauté, stirring frequently, until the potatoes are cooked, approximately 20 minutes. Cool completely.
2. Toss gently with the remaining ingredients. Refrigerate until 1 hour before serving.

Serves 4 to 6

Prominent Tastes: *Astringent, Pungent, Sour*	
If you want to reduce	eat
VATA	MORE
PITTA	LESS
KAPHA	SOME

Salad Dressings

◆

Our salad dressings are mostly low- or nonfat, providing a variety of tastes. Be sure to keep the oils and other ingredients for each dosha on hand, since many of the dressings are dosha specific.

BASIC CREAMY TOFU DRESSING

BASIC MISO DRESSING

POPPY SEED DRESSING

MINTED CITRUS DRESSING

MUSTARD DRESSING

YOGURT DILL DRESSING

LEMON-LIME DRESSING

❤ Basic Creamy Tofu Dressing

◆

Add herbs and spices to create individual flavors.

15 minutes to prepare

For Vata

2-inch piece of firm tofu *(sweet, astringent)*
1 tablespoon honey *(sweet)*
1 tablespoon Bragg's Liquid Aminos *(astringent, salty)*
1 tablespoon lemon juice *(sweet, sour)*
½ cup orange juice *(sweet, sour)*

For Pitta

2-inch piece of firm tofu *(sweet, astringent)*
1 tablespoon Sucanat *(sweet)*
1 tablespoon Bragg's Liquid Aminos *(astringent, salty)*

1 tablespoon unfiltered apple juice *(sour)*
½ cup orange juice *(sweet, astringent)*

For Kapha

1-inch piece of firm tofu *(sweet, astringent)*
1 tablespoon honey *(sweet)*
1 tablespoon Bragg's Liquid Aminos *(astringent, salty)*
1 tablespoon lemon juice *(sweet, sour)*
½ cup unfiltered apple juice *(sweet, astringent)*

Place the ingredients in a blender or food processor and blend. The dressing can be stored in the refrigerator for several days.

Makes about ³/₄ cup

Prominent Tastes: *Sweet, Sour*	
If you want to reduce	eat
VATA	SOME
PITTA	SOME
KAPHA	SOME

❧ BASIC MISO DRESSING
◆

This is a dressing for all seasons, for all doshas.

15 minutes to prepare

For Vata

1 tablespoon white miso paste *(astringent)*

1 tablespoon honey *(sweet)*

1 tablespoon Bragg's Liquid Aminos *(astringent, salty)*

1 tablespoon lemon juice *(sweet, sour)*

½ cup orange juice *(sweet, sour)*

For Pitta

2 tablespoons white miso paste *(astringent)*

1 tablespoon Sucanat *(sweet)*

1 tablespoon Bragg's Liquid Aminos *(astringent, salty)*

1 tablespoon unfiltered apple juice *(sweet, sour)*

½ cup orange juice *(sweet, sour)*

For Kapha

2 tablespoons white miso paste *(astringent)*

1 tablespoon honey *(sweet)*

1 tablespoon Bragg's Liquid Aminos *(astringent, salty)*

1 tablespoon lemon juice *(sweet, sour)*

½ cup unfiltered apple juice *(sweet, sour)*

Place the ingredients in a blender or food processor and blend. The dressing can be stored in the refrigerator for several days.

Makes about ³/₄ cup

Prominent Tastes: *Sweet, Astringent, Sour*	
If you want to reduce	*eat*
VATA	SOME
PITTA	SOME
KAPHA	SOME

❤ Poppy Seed Dressing
◆

Try Poppy Seed Dressing on a papaya or other fruit.

15 minutes to prepare

For Vata

1 tablespoon Dijon mustard *(pungent)*
1 tablespoon olive oil *(sweet)*
1 tablespoon honey *(sweet)*
1 tablespoon Bragg's Liquid Aminos *(astringent, salty)*
1 tablespoon lemon juice *(sweet, sour)*
½ cup orange juice *(sweet, sour)*
¼ cup plain nonfat yogurt *(sweet, sour)*
1 tablespoon poppy seeds *(pungent, astringent, sweet)*

For Pitta

1 tablespoon Dijon mustard *(pungent)*
1 tablespoon olive oil *(sweet)*
1 tablespoon Sucanat *(sweet)*
1 tablespoon Bragg's Liquid Aminos *(astringent, salty)*
1 tablespoon apple juice *(sweet, sour)*
½ cup orange juice *(sweet, sour)*
¼ cup plain nonfat yogurt *(sweet, sour)*
1 tablespoon poppy seeds *(pungent, astringent, sweet)*

For Kapha

1 tablespoon Dijon mustard *(pungent)*
1 tablespoon almond oil *(sweet)*
1 tablespoon honey *(sweet)*
1 tablespoon Bragg's Liquid Aminos *(astringent, salty)*
1 tablespoon lemon juice *(sweet, sour)*
½ cup unfiltered apple juice *(sweet, sour)*
¼ cup plain nonfat yogurt *(sweet, sour)*
1 tablespoon poppy seeds *(pungent, astringent, sweet)*

Combine all the ingredients in a small jar and shake well. The dressing can be stored in the refrigerator for several days.

Makes about ³/₄ cup

Prominent Tastes: *Pungent, Sweet, Sour*	
If you want to reduce	*eat*
VATA	SOME
PITTA	SOME
KAPHA	SOME

ℳINTED ℭITRUS ᗡRESSING

◆

This is a tangy, cooling dressing.

15 minutes to prepare

Juice of 4 lemons *(sour, astringent)*

Juice of 2 oranges *(sweet, sour)*

2 tablespoons honey, Sucanat, or turbinado sugar *(sweet)*

3 tablespoons Bragg's Liquid Aminos *(astringent, salty)*

1 tablespoon olive oil *(sweet)*

2 tablespoons crushed dried mint or 1 tablespoon minced fresh mint *(pungent)*

Place all the ingredients in a jar and shake. The dressing can be stored in the refrigerator for several days.

Makes about 1 cup

Prominent Tastes: *Sweet, Sour*	
If you want to reduce	*eat*
VATA	MORE
PITTA	SOME
KAPHA	LESS

♥ Mustard Dressing
◆

This dressing is great on salads, potatoes, or cooked vegetables.

15 minutes to prepare

For Vata

2 tablespoons Dijon mustard
(*pungent*)
1 tablespoon olive oil (*sweet*)
1 tablespoon honey (*sweet*)
1 tablespoon Bragg's Liquid
Aminos (*astringent, salty*)
1 tablespoon lemon juice (*sweet,
sour*)
½ cup orange juice (*sweet, sour*)

For Pitta

2 tablespoons Dijon mustard
(*pungent*)
1 tablespoon olive oil (*sweet*)
1 tablespoon Sucanat (*sweet*)
1 tablespoon Bragg's Liquid
Aminos (*astringent, salty*)
1 tablespoon apple juice (*sweet, sour*)
½ cup orange juice (*sweet, sour*)

For Kapha

2 tablespoons Dijon mustard
(*pungent*)
1 tablespoon almond oil (*sweet*)
1 tablespoon honey (*sweet*)
1 tablespoon Bragg's Liquid
Aminos (*astringent, salty*)
1 tablespoon lemon juice (*sweet,
sour*)
½ cup unfiltered apple juice (*sweet,
sour*)

Combine all ingredients in a jar and shake well. The dressing can be stored in the refrigerator for several days.

Makes about ³/₄ cup

Prominent Tastes: *Pungent, Sweet, Sour*	
If you want to reduce	*eat*
VATA	SOME
PITTA	SOME
KAPHA	SOME

❤ YOGURT DILL DRESSING

❖

15 minutes to prepare

For Vata

1 tablespoon olive oil *(sweet)*
1 tablespoon honey *(sweet)*
1 tablespoon Bragg's Liquid Aminos *(astringent, salty)*
1 tablespoon lemon juice *(sweet, sour)*
½ cup orange juice *(sweet, sour)*
¼ cup plain nonfat yogurt *(sweet, sour)*
2 tablespoons minced fresh dill *(pungent)*

For Pitta

1 tablespoon olive oil *(sweet)*
1 tablespoon Sucanat *(sweet)*
1 tablespoon Bragg's Liquid Aminos *(astringent, salty)*
1 tablespoon unfiltered apple juice *(sweet, sour)*
½ cup orange juice *(sweet, sour)*
¼ cup plain nonfat yogurt *(sweet, sour)*
2 tablespoons minced fresh dill *(pungent)*

For Kapha

1 tablespoon sunflower oil *(sweet)*
1 tablespoon honey *(sweet)*
1 tablespoon Bragg's Liquid Aminos *(astringent, salty)*
1 tablespoon lemon juice *(sweet, sour)*
½ cup unfiltered apple juice *(sweet, sour)*
¼ cup plain nonfat yogurt *(sweet, sour)*
2 tablespoons minced fresh dill *(pungent)*

Combine all the ingredients in a small jar and shake well. The dressing can be stored in the refrigerator for several days.

Makes about ¾ cup

Prominent Tastes: *Sweet, Sour, Astringent*	
If you want to reduce	*eat*
VATA	SOME
PITTA	SOME
KAPHA	SOME

LEMON-LIME DRESSING

◆

15 minutes to prepare

For Vata

1 tablespoon olive oil *(sweet)*
1 tablespoon honey *(sweet)*
1 tablespoon Bragg's Liquid
    Aminos *(astringent, salty)*
1 tablespoon lemon juice *(sweet,
    sour)*
½ cup lime juice *(sweet, sour)*

For Pitta

1 tablespoon olive oil
1 tablespoon Sucanat
1 tablespoon Bragg's Liquid
    Aminos *(astringent, salty)*

1 tablespoon lemon juice *(sweet,
    sour)*
½ cup lime juice *(sweet, sour)*

For Kapha

1 tablespoon sunflower oil *(sweet)*
1 tablespoon honey *(sweet)*
1 tablespoon Bragg's Liquid
    Aminos *(astringent, salty)*
1 tablespoon lemon juice *(sweet,
    sour)*
½ cup lime juice *(sweet, sour)*

Combine all the ingredients in a small jar and shake well. The dressing can be stored in the refrigerator for several days.

Makes about 1 cup

Prominent Tastes: *Sweet, Sour*	
If you want to reduce	*eat*
VATA	SOME
PITTA	SOME
KAPHA	SOME

&NTRÉES

◆

Our entrées, or main dishes, offer variety without restricting you to Indian food, although we use many Ayurvedic spices and herbs. Combined with certain side dishes, salads, and breads (see chapter 7, Menu Planning), these dishes help provide nutritional balance. Pass the *churans* to your family and friends for further doshic satisfaction.

Most of these dishes are easy to prepare. Preparation time is approximate, allowing for individual variation.

PASTA WITH MADEIRA
MUSHROOM SAUCE

CARROT CROQUETTES
WITH CURRANT SAUCE

A DIFFERENT PESTO

CHEESELESS LASAGNE

MUSHROOM
STROGANOFF

PIZZA

SPINACH PIZZA
RUSTICA

POTATO-LEEK FRITTATA

VEGETABLE BARLEY
CASSEROLE

TOFU SATAY

VEGETABLE CHOW MEIN

VEGETABLE TOFU
CRUSTLESS PIE

VEGETABLE PANEER
TART

VEGETABLE STRUDEL

BAKED WINTER SQUASH
WITH WILD RICE–
CRANBERRY STUFFING

VEGGIE BURGERS

COSMIC CURRY

COSMIC CURRY
ENCHILADAS

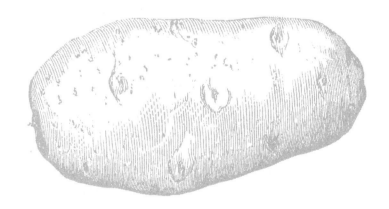

♥Pasta with Madeira Mushroom Sauce

◆

Light and fast, this is great for surprise guests.
Don't worry, the alcohol burns off.

20 minutes to prepare

1 teaspoon olive oil *(sweet)*
1 large portobello mushroom,
  sliced *(sweet, astringent)*
10 shiitake mushrooms, sliced
  (sweet, astringent)
20 domestic mushrooms, sliced
  (sweet, astringent)
1 garlic clove, minced *(all but sour)*

2 tablespoons minced scallions
  (pungent, sweet)
½ cup chopped fresh parsley
  (pungent, astringent)
Sea salt *(salty)* and pepper *(pungent)*
¼ cup Madeira wine *(sweet)*
2 cups cooked pasta of your choice
  (sweet)

1. In a skillet, heat the oil to the smoking point. Sauté the mushrooms, garlic, and scallions for 2 minutes, stirring frequently.
2. When browned, add the parsley and salt and pepper to taste. Add the Madeira and cook for 2 minutes.
3. Toss with the cooked pasta.

Serves 2 to 4

Prominent Tastes: *Sweet, Astringent*	
If you want to reduce	*eat*
VATA	MORE
PITTA	SOME
KAPHA	LESS

CARROT CROQUETTES WITH CURRANT SAUCE

◆

These are lovely with spinach on the side. **Pittas,** *don't overeat!*

30 minutes to prepare

2 cups shredded carrots *(sweet, pungent)*

½ cup minced celery *(bitter, astringent)*

2 cups cooked rice *(sweet)*

½ cup bread crumbs plus extra, for rolling *(sweet)*

2 eggs *(sweet)*

½ cup raisins *(sweet)*

4 tablespoons Bragg's Liquid Aminos *(astringent, salty)*

1 tablespoon Vegit *(all)*

Currant Sauce (recipe follows)

1. Preheat the oven to 350°F.
2. Combine all the ingredients except the extra bread crumbs and the Currant Sauce in a mixing bowl. Shape into croquettes or patties and roll in the bread crumbs.
3. Bake for about 30 minutes. Serve with the Currant Sauce.

CURRANT SAUCE

1 small jar currant jelly *(sweet)*

2 tablespoons cornstarch dissolved in 2 cups orange juice *(sweet, sour)*

1 cup currants *(sweet)*

Combine all the ingredients in a saucepan. Bring to a boil to thicken. Serve the warm sauce over the croquettes.

Serves 4 to 6

Prominent Taste: *Sweet*	
If you want to reduce	*eat*
VATA	MORE
PITTA	MORE
KAPHA	LESS

A DIFFERENT PESTO

◆

*Made without cheese or added oil, this is a
yummy version of an old classic.*

20 minutes to prepare

2 bunches fresh spinach *(bitter)*

2 avocados, cut into pieces *(sweet)*

2 bunches fresh cilantro *(pungent)*

2 bunches fresh parsley *(pungent, astringent)*

2 bunches fresh basil *(pungent)*

Juice of 1 lemon *(sour, astringent)*

½ cup pine nuts *(sweet)*

Sea salt *(salty)*

Pepper *(pungent)*

4 cups cooked pasta of your choice *(sweet)*

Combine all the ingredients in a food processor and blend well. Add some water to aid in mixing, if needed. Toss with warm pasta.

Serves 4 to 6

Prominent Tastes: *All*	
If you want to reduce	*eat*
VATA	SOME
PITTA	SOME
KAPHA	SOME

♥CHEESELESS LASAGNE

◆

This is a hearty, cheeseless version of an old favorite. Sun-dried tomatoes replace tomato sauce for a less sour flavor.

1 hour to prepare

Sauce

1 teaspoon ghee *(sweet)*

6 carrots, cut into 1-inch pieces *(sweet, pungent)*

6 zucchini, cut into 1-inch pieces *(sweet)*

6 celery stalks, cut into 1-inch pieces *(bitter, astringent)*

1 bunch parsley *(pungent, astringent)*

1 16-ounce jar sun-dried tomatoes, drained *(sweet, sour)*

1 tablespoon oregano *(pungent)*

Dash of sea salt *(salty)*

⅛ teaspoon Italian seasoning *(pungent)*

Filling

1 pound firm tofu, crumbled *(sweet, astringent)*

1 to 1½ cups sauce (from step 1)

½ cup ground pine nuts *(sweet)*

1 package spinach lasagna noodles, cooked and drained *(bitter, sweet)*

Bread crumbs *(sweet)*

1. In a large sauté pan, heat the ghee to the smoking point. Sauté the carrots, zucchini, and celery in the ghee for 5 minutes. Combine with the parsley, tomatoes, oregano, salt, and Italian seasoning and grind coarsely in a food processor. Return to the pot and simmer for 5 minutes. Remove from heat and set aside while you prepare the filling.
2. Preheat the oven to 350°F.
3. Combine the tofu, sauce, and nuts.
4. Layer in the casserole dish as follows: sauce, noodles, filling, sauce, noodles, filling, sauce, noodles, sauce, bread crumbs.
5. Bake, uncovered, for 40 minutes, or until the bread crumbs are golden and the lasagne is bubbling.

Serves 8 to 10

Prominent Tastes: *Sweet, Astringent, Pungent*	
If you want to reduce	*eat*
VATA	MORE
PITTA	SOME
KAPHA	SOME

♥ MUSHROOM STROGANOFF

◆

Beef Stroganoff was never this good.

25 minutes to prepare

1 large portobello mushroom *(sweet, astringent)*

10 shiitake mushrooms *(sweet, astringent)*

1 pound domestic mushrooms *(sweet, astringent)*

1 teaspoon olive oil *(sweet)*

1 garlic clove, minced *(all but sour)*

½ yellow onion, chopped *(pungent, sweet)*

1 tablespoon Bragg's Liquid Aminos *(astringent, salty)*

1 tablespoon vegetable broth powder *(all)*

1 tablespoon cornstarch mixed with ½ cup water *(sweet)*

½ cup plain nonfat yogurt *(sweet, sour)*

1 teaspoon tarragon *(pungent)*

2 tablespoons chopped fresh parsley *(pungent, astringent)*

Dash of grated nutmeg *(pungent)*

2 cups cooked basmati rice or 2 cups cooked pasta of your choice *(sweet)*

Fresh parsley sprigs *(pungent, astringent)*

1. Cut all the mushrooms into bite-size pieces, using most of the stems.
2. In a large skillet, heat the oil to the smoking point. Add the mushrooms, garlic, and onion. Sauté for 5 minutes, until the mushrooms are browned.

3. Add the remaining ingredients except the rice or pasta and parsley sprigs and simmer for 1 minute, until thickened.
4. Serve over rice or pasta and garnish with the parsley sprigs.

Serves 4 to 6

Prominent Tastes: *Sweet, Pungent, Astringent*	
If you want to reduce	*eat*
VATA	MORE
PITTA	SOME
KAPHA	LESS

♥𝒫IZZA

◆

Be creative with this: Provide a variety of vegetables and allow each person to build the perfect personal pizza for his or her body type.

1¹/₂ hours to prepare

Pizza Dough

1 cup warm water
1 tablespoon yeast
1 tablespoon turbinado sugar *(sweet)*

2½ to 3 cups organic unbleached white flour or 2 cups white and 1 cup organic whole wheat pastry flour *(sweet, astringent)*
2 tablespoons olive oil *(sweet)*
½ teaspoon sea salt *(salty)*

1. Combine the water, yeast, sugar, and half the flour in a large bowl. Mix well. Add the oil and salt. Gradually add the rest of the flour. Mix with a large wooden spoon until a soft dough is achieved.

2. Place the dough on a lightly floured surface and knead 5 minutes. If the dough is too sticky, sprinkle with extra flour. Place the dough in a lightly oiled bowl and let rise until doubled, about 45 minutes.

3. After the dough has risen, place on a lightly floured surface and divide into 2 equal parts. Cover with a towel and let stand for 20 minutes. Shape into 4 mini pizzas or 1 large pizza.

4. Preheat the oven to 400° F.

5. Top the pizza with:

   Muir Glen Organic Pizza Sauce

   Oregano or Italian seasonings

   Shredded vegetables of your choice

   Grated Parmesan cheese, optional

6. Bake for 20 minutes, or until the crust is golden.

Makes 4 mini pizzas or 1 large pizza

Prominent Taste: *Sweet*	
If you want to reduce	*eat*
VATA	MORE
PITTA	SOME
KAPHA	SOME

SPINACH PIZZA RUSTICA

◆

This is a filling main dish for a special luncheon.
Serve with a green salad.

2 hours to prepare

2 teaspoons ghee or olive oil *(sweet)*

2 large leeks, chopped and well
washed *(pungent, sweet)*

2 pounds spinach, washed and
chopped *(bitter)*

5 medium Yukon Gold potatoes,
chopped *(astringent)*

2 eggs, beaten *(sweet)*

1 teaspoon sea salt *(salty)*

¼ teaspoon tarragon *(pungent)*

½ cup chopped walnuts or
pine nuts *(sweet)*

Pizza Rustica Dough

4 cups organic unbleached white
flour or organic whole wheat
pastry flour *(sweet, astringent)*

1 teaspoon turbinado sugar *(sweet)*

1 teaspoon sea salt *(salty)*

½ cup (1 stick) cold butter, cut into
bits *(sweet)*

4 large eggs, beaten *(sweet)*

Egg wash made from 1 egg beaten
with 2 tablespoons water *(sweet)*

Bread crumbs *(sweet)*

1. In a large skillet, heat 1 teaspoon ghee or oil to the smoking point. Sauté
   the leeks until browned. Add the spinach and continue cooking until
   the spinach is wilted. Place in a bowl.

2. Heat the skillet again, add the remaining 1 teaspoon ghee or oil, and
   sauté the potatoes until browned, about 15 minutes. Place in the bowl
   with the spinach and leeks. Toss with the eggs, salt, tarragon, and walnuts or pine nuts. Cool.

3. Preheat the oven to 375° F.

4. Make the Pizza Rustica Dough: Place the dry ingredients in a food
   processor and blend. Add the butter and pulse until the mixture resembles coarse meal. Add the eggs and pulse until the eggs are incorporated
   and the dough is formed. Don't overprocess. Wrap the dough in plastic
   and chill for 1 hour.

5. Roll the dough into a large circle on a floured surface. Place in a large cake pan, pizza pan, or pie tin and spoon in the filling. Fold over the edges of dough and brush with the egg wash. Sprinkle with the bread crumbs.

6. Bake for about 1 hour, or until the crust is golden brown. (The dough can be made ahead and chilled in the pan, covered.) Serve warm or at room temperature.

Serves 6 to 8

Prominent Tastes: *Sweet, Astringent, Bitter*	
If you want to reduce	*eat*
VATA	SOME
PITTA	SOME
KAPHA	SOME

$\mathcal{P}$OTATO-$\mathcal{L}$EEK $\mathcal{F}$RITTATA

◆

Yellow Finn or Yukon Gold potatoes add a special quality to this dish, but regular white potatoes may also be used.

1¹/₂ hours to prepare

1 teaspoon ghee *(sweet)*

1 large leek, diced and washed thoroughly *(pungent, sweet)*

1 pound Yellow Finn or Yukon Gold potatoes, diced *(astringent)*

4 eggs, beaten *(sweet)*

2 tablespoons vegetable broth powder *(all)*

1 tablespoon Bragg's Liquid Aminos *(astringent, salty)*

¹/₂ teaspoon thyme *(pungent)*

¹/₂ teaspoon tarragon *(pungent)*

¹/₂ cup plus 2 tablespoons ground pine nuts *(sweet)*

1. Preheat the oven to 350° F.
2. In a skillet, heat ¹/₂ teaspoon ghee to the smoking point. Add the leek and cook until softened, about 5 minutes. Remove and place in a bowl.
3. Heat the remaining ¹/₂ teaspoon ghee in the skillet to the smoking point. Add the potatoes and cook, stirring frequently, until browned and cooked but still firm. Combine with the remaining ingredients except the 2 tablespoons pine nuts.
4. Pour into an oiled or sprayed 9 × 12-inch baking dish and top with the remaining pine nuts. Bake, uncovered, for 30 to 40 minutes. Serve warm.

Serves 6 to 8

Prominent Tastes: *Sweet, Pungent, Astringent*	
If you want to reduce	*eat*
VATA	SOME
PITTA	SOME
KAPHA	SOME

♥ᵁEGETABLE ℬARLEY 𝒞ASSEROLE

◆

1¹/₂ hours to prepare

3 cups bite-size vegetables, such as carrots *(sweet, pungent)*, zucchini *(sweet)*, yellow squash *(sweet)*, potatoes *(astringent)*, and leeks *(pungent, sweet)*

1 tablespoon ghee *(sweet)*

3 cups cooked barley *(sweet)*

1 cup fresh or frozen corn (if using frozen corn, choose organic if possible and thaw) *(sweet)*

1 cup fresh or frozen peas (if using frozen peas, choose organic if possible and thaw) *(sweet, astringent)*

2 tablespoons thyme *(pungent)*

1 tablespoon oregano *(pungent)*

4 tablespoons Bragg's Liquid Aminos *(astringent, salty)*

3 tablespoons vegetable broth powder *(all)*

1 cup Muir Glen Organic Tomato Sauce *(sweet, sour)*

2 tablespoons arrowroot dissolved in ¹/₂ cup water

Bread crumbs, for topping *(sweet)*

1. Preheat the oven to 350°F.
2. In a large skillet, sauté the bite-size vegetables in the ghee. Combine with the rest of the ingredients except the bread crumbs.
3. Pour into an oiled 9 × 12-inch casserole dish and sprinkle liberally with the bread crumbs. Bake for about 40 minutes, or until bubbling.

Serves 8 to 10

Prominent Tastes: *Sweet, Astringent*	
If you want to reduce	*eat*
VATA	SOME
PITTA	MORE
KAPHA	MORE

Tofu Satay

◆

Who needs chicken? This warm, spicy dish is sooo good,
you'll be back for more.

1 hour to prepare

1 brick hard style tofu *(sweet,*
astringent)

2 tablespoons vegetable broth
powder *(all)*

1 tablespoon Bragg's Liquid
Aminos *(astringent, salty)*

1-inch piece of fresh gingerroot,
peeled and smashed *(pungent,*
sweet)

1 tablespoon sesame oil *(sweet)*

Satay Sauce

1 garlic clove, optional *(all but sour)*

¼ cup peanut butter *(sweet,*
astringent)

¼ cup orange juice *(sweet, sour)*

1 can (14 ounces) light coconut
milk *(sweet)*

1 teaspoon Thai-style chili paste
(pungent)

2 tablespoons dried onion flakes
(pungent, sweet)

3 tablespoons Bragg's Liquid
Aminos *(astringent, salty)*

1 2-ounce bottle Thai Kitchen
Satay Sauce *(pungent)*

¼ cup chopped fresh cilantro
(pungent)

3 cups cooked basmati rice *(sweet)*

Fresh cilantro sprigs *(pungent)* and
thin lemon slices *(sour,*
astringent), for garnish

1. Press the tofu between layers of paper toweling. Place 1 plate on each
   side of the toweling and press down to express as much liquid from the
   tofu as possible. Cut the tofu into 1-inch cubes.
2. Bring 3 cups of water, the vegetable broth powder, the tablespoon of
   Bragg's Liquid Aminos, and ginger to a boil. Immerse the tofu cubes in
   this broth and simmer 15 minutes. Drain but save the broth.
3. Heat the sesame oil in a skillet and sauté the tofu, turning often to
   brown all sides. (Or place on wooden skewers and grill with other vegetables.) Drain well on a paper towel.

4. Combine all the sauce ingredients except the cilantro in a food processor and process until smooth, adding the reserved broth as needed to create a gravylike consistency. Heat through, then add the cilantro.
5. Serve over rice and garnish with the cilantro sprigs and lemon slices.

Serves 6 to 8

Prominent Tastes: *Pungent, Astringent*	
If you want to reduce	*eat*
VATA	SOME
PITTA	MORE
KAPHA	SOME

VEGETABLE CHOW MEIN

◆

When you master Chinese cooking, the variations are endless.

40 minutes to prepare

1 leek, washed thoroughly *(pungent, sweet)*

2 carrots *(sweet, pungent)*

2 zucchini *(sweet)*

2 celery stalks *(bitter, astringent)*

1 garlic clove, minced *(all but sour)*

2-inch piece of fresh gingerroot, peeled and minced or grated *(pungent, sweet)*

2 tablespoons dark toasted sesame oil *(sweet)*

1 can (7½ ounces) sliced water chestnuts, optional *(sweet)*

¼ pound mushrooms, sliced *(sweet, astringent)*

1 pound firm tofu, drained and cut into 1-inch pieces *(sweet, astringent)*

1 pound fresh Chinese noodles *(sweet)*

¼ cup finely chopped fresh cilantro *(pungent)*

1. Slice the leek, carrots, zucchini, and celery into bite-size pieces.
2. In a wok or skillet, sauté the garlic and ginger in 1 tablespoon hot sesame oil. Keeping the temperature high, add the leek, carrots, zucchini, celery, and optional water chestnuts. Stir-fry quickly, then remove from the pan.
3. Adding a little more oil if necessary, stir-fry the mushrooms and tofu until browned on all sides. Remove from the pan and drain well.
4. While you are stir-frying, cook the noodles according to package directions. Rinse well in cold water until completely cool and drain well. Panfry in a hot, lightly oiled wok or skillet until browned. (Constant stirring and scraping is necessary to prevent the noodles from sticking to the bottom of the pan.)
5. Toss the vegetables, cilantro, and noodles together and serve.

Serves 4 to 6

Prominent Tastes: *Sweet, Pungent*	
If you want to reduce	*eat*
VATA	SOME
PITTA	SOME
KAPHA	SOME

Vegetable Tofu Crustless Pie

◆

*This takes just a few minutes to prepare and is great
for a quick dinner after work.*

50 minutes to prepare

1 large leek, washed, cut into
pieces, and washed again
(pungent, sweet)

1 cup sliced carrots *(sweet, pungent)*

1 pound spinach *(bitter)*

1 cup toasted pine nuts *(sweet)*

1 pound firm tofu *(sweet,
astringent)*

2 tablespoons Bragg's Liquid
Aminos *(astringent, salty)*

1 teaspoon tarragon *(pungent)*

⅛ teaspoon grated nutmeg
(pungent, astringent)

4 eggs *(sweet)*

½ cup dry bread crumbs *(sweet)*

2 tablespoons sesame seeds *(sweet)*

1. Preheat the oven to 400° F.
2. Place the leek, carrots, spinach, pine nuts, and tofu, one kind at a time,
   in a food processor and process until finely ground or chopped.
3. In a dry nonstick pan, sauté the leek-carrot-spinach mixture for 2 minutes. Combine with all the remaining ingredients except the sesame seeds.
4. Pour into an oiled or sprayed 9 × 12-inch baking dish. Sprinkle with
   the sesame seeds and bake, uncovered, for 30 minutes.

Serves 6 to 8

Prominent Tastes: *Sweet, Pungent, Astringent*	
If you want to reduce	*eat*
VATA	MORE
PITTA	SOME
KAPHA	LESS

VEGETABLE PANEER TART

◆

Different combinations of vegetables make this dish uniquely satisfying to each dosha.

45 minutes to prepare

5 cups mixed vegetables, such as 2 leeks *(pungent, sweet)*, 1 broccoli stalk *(bitter, astringent)*, 2 celery stalks *(bitter, astringent)*, ½ cup green beans *(sweet, astringent)*, ½ yellow pepper *(sweet, astringent)*, ½ pound mushrooms *(sweet, astringent)*, or 1 cup fresh peas *(sweet, astringent)*

2 tablespoons ghee or oil *(sweet)*

½ cup paneer cheese *(sweet, sour)*

2 eggs *(sweet)*

Pinch of tarragon *(pungent)*

Pinch of sea salt *(salty)*

2 tablespoons Bragg's Liquid Aminos *(astringent, salty)*

1 recipe Pastry Dough (recipe follows)

½ cup bread crumbs *(sweet)*

1. Preheat the oven to 400°F.
2. Chop all the vegetables except the peas into small pieces. In a skillet, sauté all the vegetables in ghee or oil until tender.
3. Mix with the cheese, eggs, tarragon, salt, and Bragg's Liquid Aminos. Pour into the pastry shell and sprinkle with the bread crumbs.
4. Bake for 40 minutes, until the center of the tart is firm and the bread crumbs are golden.

PASTRY DOUGH

4 cups organic unbleached white flour *(sweet, astringent)*

½ teaspoon sea salt *(salty)*

2 sticks cold, unsalted butter, cut into pieces *(sweet)*

½ cup vegetable shortening *(sweet)*

¾ to 1 cup ice-cold orange juice *(sweet, sour)*

1. Place the flour, salt, butter, and shortening in the food processor and process until mealy. Slowly pour in the orange juice until the dough begins to hold together.
2. Wrap the dough in plastic wrap and refrigerate for 30 minutes.
3. Roll out half of the dough on a floured surface to form a shell. Place in a tart pan. The remaining dough can be stored in the refrigerator for several days.

Serves 4 to 6

Prominent Tastes: *Sweet, Astringent, Bitter*	
If you want to reduce	*eat*
VATA	SOME
PITTA	MORE
KAPHA	LESS

VEGETABLE STRUDEL

◆

The vegetables you use in this dish can be determined by your doshic requirements.

45 minutes to 1 hour to prepare

5 cups mixed fresh vegetables, such as potatoes *(astringent)*, carrots *(sweet, pungent)*, and zucchini *(sweet)*, cut into bite-size pieces

1 tablespoon ghee *(sweet)*

½ package organic frozen corn *(sweet)*

½ package organic frozen peas *(sweet, astringent)*

2 tablespoons vegetable broth powder *(all)*

½ teaspoon thyme *(pungent)*

½ tablespoon tarragon *(pungent)*

½ tablespoon oregano *(pungent)*

½ tablespoon rosemary *(pungent, bitter)*

¼ teaspoon sea salt *(salty)*

2 tablespoons Bragg's Liquid Aminos *(astringent, salty)*

1 tablespoon cornstarch *(sweet)*

1 package frozen Pepperidge Farm Puff Pastry, thawed *(sweet)*

Egg wash made from 1 egg beaten with 1 tablespoon water *(sweet)*

Sesame seeds *(sweet)*

Dried parsley *(pungent, astringent)*

1. In a large skillet, sauté the fresh vegetables in the ghee until tender. Add the frozen corn and peas, the broth powder, the herbs, the salt, the Bragg's Liquid Aminos, and the cornstarch and toss. Cool.
2. Preheat the oven to 400° F.
3. On a floured surface, roll out the defrosted puff pastry into a large rectangle. Place the cooled filling onto the pastry at one end and fold over the sides. Moisten the edges with water. Roll up into a burrito-like shape. Brush with the egg wash and sprinkle with sesame seeds and dried parsley.
4. Bake about 45 minutes. Serve immediately.

Serves 6 to 8

Prominent Taste: *Balanced*	
If you want to reduce	*eat*
VATA	SOME
PITTA	SOME
KAPHA	SOME

♥Baked Winter Squash with Wild Rice-Cranberry Stuffing

◆

Warm and filling, this can be put together in the morning and baked before dinner.

1½ hours to prepare

2 medium winter squash, such as kabocha, acorn, golden nugget, or butternut *(sweet)*

1 cup orange juice *(sweet, sour)*

1 cup wild rice *(sweet)*

Pinch of sea salt *(salty)*

½ cup toasted pine nuts *(sweet)*

¼ cup dried cranberries *(astringent, sweet)*

1 tablespoon dried onion flakes *(pungent, sweet)*

1 teaspoon grated orange zest *(bitter)*

1 tablespoon Bragg's Liquid Aminos *(astringent, salty)*

1 teaspoon dried sage *(pungent, astringent)*

2 tablespoons bread crumbs *(sweet)*

1. Preheat the oven to 350° F.
2. Split the squash in half lengthwise. Remove the seeds and stringy pulp with a large spoon. Place the squash halves in a baking dish with the orange juice, cover, and bake for 45 minutes, until cooked through but still firm. Reserve the juice.
3. Bring 2 cups of water to a boil. Add the rice and salt and simmer for 30 to 40 minutes, until the rice is fluffy.

4. Combine the rice with all the remaining ingredients except the bread crumbs. Add the reserved orange juice. Mound this mixture in the hollow of the squash and sprinkle with the bread crumbs.

5. Bake for 30 minutes, until heated through and the bread crumbs are browned.

Serves 4

Prominent Tastes: *Sweet, Pungent, Astringent*	
If you want to reduce	*eat*
VATA	SOME
PITTA	SOME
KAPHA	LESS

$\mathcal{V}$EGGIE $\mathcal{B}$URGERS

◆

The recipe for these uniquely satisfying patties makes enough for a party.

1½ hours to prepare

⅔ cup pearl barley *(sweet)*

⅔ cup brown lentils *(sweet, astringent)*

⅔ cup basmati rice *(sweet)*

2 cups grated carrots *(sweet, pungent)*

1 cup chopped celery *(bitter, astringent)*

¼ cup vegetable oil plus additional, for frying *(sweet)*

¼ cup sunflower seeds *(sweet)*

1 tablespoon chopped fresh basil or 1 teaspoon dried *(pungent)*

2 teaspoons chopped fresh thyme or 1 teaspoon dried *(pungent)*

2 teaspoons chopped fresh oregano or 1 teaspoon dried *(pungent)*

Sea salt *(salty)*

Pepper *(pungent)*

4 large eggs, beaten *(sweet)*

7 tablespoons flour *(sweet)*

1. Bring 3 cups of water to a boil in a heavy pot. Stir in the barley, lentils, and rice. Cover and cook until the grains are tender, about 40 minutes. Drain, transfer to a large bowl, cool completely.
2. In a skillet, sauté the carrots and celery in the ¼ cup of vegetable oil until tender, about 12 minutes. Add to the grains and let cool. Mix in the seasonings and salt and pepper to taste.
3. Stir the beaten eggs and flour into the mixture. Press ¼ cup of the mixture between the palms of your hands to form patties.
4. Heat additional oil in a large heavy skillet. Add patties in batches and cook until golden brown, about 5 minutes on each side. Serve on wheat buns.

Serves 12 to 14

Prominent Tastes: *Sweet, Pungent*	
If you want to reduce	*eat*
VATA	MORE
PITTA	SOME
KAPHA	LESS

Cosmic Curry

◆

Choose your own vegetables to make this dish uniquely yours.

45 minutes to prepare

1 sweet potato, peeled and cubed (leave out for **Kaphas**) *(sweet)*

1 cup diced carrots *(sweet, pungent)*

½ cup diced leeks, washed well *(pungent, sweet)*

½ cup diced cauliflower *(sweet, astringent)*

2 tablespoons ghee *(sweet)*

3 roma tomatoes, quartered *(sweet, sour)*

1 pound spinach, washed and stemmed *(bitter)*

1½ cups light coconut milk *(sweet)*

1 tablespoon grated fresh gingerroot *(pungent, sweet)*

1 tablespoon ground cumin seeds *(pungent)*

2 teaspoons coriander *(pungent, bitter)*

1 teaspoon cinnamon *(pungent, bitter)*

½ teaspoon turmeric *(bitter, pungent, astringent)*

⅛ teaspoon ground cardamom *(pungent, sweet)*

1 tablespoon lemongrass *(pungent, sour)*

4 tablespoons Bragg's Liquid Aminos *(astringent, salty)*

1 tablespoon vegetable broth powder *(all)*

Pinch of sea salt *(salty)*

4 cups cooked basmati rice *(sweet)*

1. In a skillet, sauté the sweet potato, carrots, leeks, and cauliflower in 1 tablespoon ghee for 10 minutes. Add the tomatoes and spinach and cook until tender, about 3 minutes.

2. Add the remaining ingredients except rice with 1 cup water and bring to a quick boil. Turn off the heat and let stand until ready to serve.

3. Reheat, if necessary, and serve over basmati rice.

Serves 6 to 8

Prominent Taste: *Balanced*	
If you want to reduce	*eat*
VATA	MORE
PITTA	MORE
KAPHA	LESS

COSMIC CURRY ENCHILADAS

◆

Using lots of spices and vegetables, these are good for every dosha.

1 hour to prepare

1 sweet potato, peeled and cubed (leave out for **Kaphas**) *(sweet)*

1 cup diced carrots *(sweet, pungent)*

1 cup chopped leeks, washed well *(pungent)*

1 cup diced cauliflower *(sweet, astringent)*

2 tablespoons ghee *(sweet)*

3 roma tomatoes, quartered *(sweet)*

1 pound spinach, washed and stemmed *(bitter)*

1 tablespoon grated fresh gingerroot *(pungent)*

1 tablespoon ground cumin seeds *(pungent)*

2 teaspoons coriander *(pungent, sweet)*

1 teaspoon cinnamon *(pungent, sweet)*

½ teaspoon turmeric *(bitter, pungent, astringent)*

⅛ teaspoon ground cardamom *(pungent, sweet)*

1 tablespoon lemongrass *(pungent, sour)*

4 tablespoons Bragg's Liquid Aminos *(astringent, salty)*

1 tablespoon vegetable broth powder *(all)*

Pinch of sea salt *(salty)*

1½ cups light coconut milk *(sweet)*

10 to 12 Whole Wheat Chappatis (page 146) *(sweet)*

¼ cup dried parsley or coriander *(pungent, astringent)*

1. Preheat the oven to 350° F.
2. In a large skillet, sauté the sweet potato, carrots, leeks, and cauliflower in 1 tablespoon ghee for 10 minutes. Add the tomatoes and spinach and cook until tender, about 3 minutes.
3. Mix the herbs, spices, Bragg's Liquid Aminos, vegetable broth powder, salt, coconut milk, and ½ cup of water in a bowl. Set aside 1 cup. Mix the rest into the vegetables.
4. Roll into the chappatis, place in an oiled baking dish, and cover with the remaining sauce. Sprinkle with parsley or coriander and bake for 20 minutes, or until bubbly.

Serves 6 to 8

Prominent Taste: *Balanced*	
If you want to reduce	*eat*
VATA	MORE
PITTA	MORE
KAPHA	SOME

SIDE DISHES

◆

Our side dishes offer interest and balance to your main event.

BARLEY PILAF

BRAISED FENNEL

COCONUT BEANS

CRACKED WHEAT PILAF

CUMINY GREENS

GLAZED CARROTS

LEEKS AND LIMAS

MINTED PEA SOUFFLÉ

MINTED RICE AND PEAS

ORANGE ALMOND RICE

ORANGE ALMOND
SPINACH

POTATO HASH

QUINOA PILAF

ROASTED MUSTARD
POTATOES

SAFFRON RICE

SWEET SWEET POTATOES

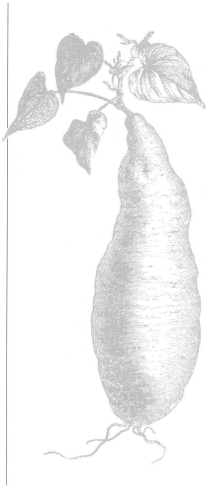

❤ BARLEY PILAF

◆

This is best for Pitta and Kapha.

1 hour to prepare

½ teaspoon sea salt *(salty)*

1 cup barley *(sweet)*

¼ teaspoon ghee or olive or sunflower oil *(sweet)*

¼ cup diced celery *(bitter, astringent)*

¼ cup diced carrots *(sweet, pungent)*

¼ cup peas *(sweet, astringent)*

1 tablespoon Bragg's Liquid Aminos *(astringent, salty)*

1 tablespoon vegetable broth powder *(all)*

1. In a saucepan, bring 3 to 4 cups of water and the salt to a boil. Add the barley and simmer for 45 minutes, or until the barley is soft and the water is absorbed.
2. In a skillet, heat the ghee or oil to the smoking point. Add the vegetables and sauté 5 minutes. Add to the cooked barley with the Bragg's Liquid Aminos and vegetable broth powder. Let stand 5 minutes before serving.

Serves 4 to 6

Prominent Tastes: *Sweet, Astringent*	
If you want to reduce	*eat*
VATA	SOME
PITTA	MORE
KAPHA	MORE

♥ℬRAISED ℱENNEL

◆

The fennel bulb is balanced with a buttery, oniony taste.

1 hour to prepare

3 fennel bulbs, stems removed
(pungent, sweet)
1 teaspoon ghee *(sweet)*

¾ cup orange juice *(sweet, sour)*
Sea salt *(salty)*
Pepper *(pungent)*

1. Cut the fennel bulbs in half.
2. Melt the ghee in a skillet. Place the fennel bulbs, cut sides down, in the skillet and sauté, covered, about 10 minutes, until golden. Add the orange juice, salt, and pepper and continue to cook for an additional 30 minutes, or until the liquid is absorbed and the fennel is soft.

Serves 2 to 4

Prominent Tastes: *Pungent, Sweet*	
If you want to reduce	*eat*
VATA	SOME
PITTA	SOME
KAPHA	SOME

Coconut Beans

◆

This is our version of an Indian specialty called Poriyal.

20 minutes to prepare

1 teaspoon olive or sunflower oil or ghee *(sweet)*

3 teaspoons brown mustard seeds *(pungent)*

3 teaspoons cumin seeds *(pungent)*

3 pounds green beans, finely chopped *(sweet, astringent)*

Sea salt *(salty)*

½ teaspoon asafoetida (hing) *(pungent)*

6 tablespoons grated coconut *(sweet)*

1 tablespoon ghee *(sweet)*

1. In a heavy saucepan, heat the oil or ghee to the smoking point. Add the mustard seeds and cumin seeds. When the seeds sputter, add the beans, salt, hing, and ¼ cup of water. Cover and simmer over low heat until the beans are tender.

2. Add the coconut and 1 tablespoon of ghee; mix well.

Serves 4 to 6

Prominent Tastes: *Sweet, Pungent*	
If you want to reduce	*eat*
VATA	SOME
PITTA	LESS
KAPHA	SOME

♥CRACKED WHEAT PILAF

♦

20 minutes to prepare

¼ teaspoon ghee or olive or sunflower oil *(sweet)*

1 cup cracked wheat *(sweet, astringent)*

½ teaspoon sea salt *(salty)*

¼ cup diced celery *(bitter, astringent)*

¼ cup diced carrots *(sweet, pungent)*

¼ cup peas *(sweet, astringent)*

1 tablespoon dried onion flakes *(pungent, sweet)*

1 tablespoon Bragg's Liquid Aminos *(astringent, salty)*

1 tablespoon vegetable broth powder *(all)*

1. In a skillet, heat the ghee or oil to the smoking point. Add the cracked wheat and salt. Stirring frequently, brown the wheat.
2. Add the celery, carrots, and peas and sauté 5 minutes.
3. Add the onion flakes, Bragg's Liquid Aminos, vegetable broth powder, and 2 cups of water. Simmer 15 minutes. Let stand 5 minutes before serving.

Serves 4 to 6

Prominent Tastes: *Sweet, Pungent, Astringent*	
If you want to reduce	eat
VATA	SOME
PITTA	SOME
KAPHA	LESS

Cuminy Greens

◆

Use any combination of greens for a satisfying, pacifying dish.

20 minutes to prepare

1 teaspoon olive oil or ghee *(sweet)*

3 teaspoons brown mustard seeds *(pungent)*

3 teaspoons cumin seeds *(pungent)*

½ teaspoon minced garlic *(all but sour)*

3 pounds greens, such as kale, chard, beet greens, or spinach *(bitter)*

Pinch of sea salt *(salty)*

1. In a heavy saucepan, heat the oil. Add the mustard seeds, cumin seeds, and garlic. When the seeds sputter, add the greens, salt, and ¼ cup of water.
2. Cover and simmer over low heat until the greens are tender, about 15 minutes.

Serves 4 to 6

Prominent Tastes: *Bitter, Pungent*	
If you want to reduce	*eat*
VATA	SOME
PITTA	SOME
KAPHA	MORE

Glazed Carrots

◆

20 minutes to prepare

2 cups cleaned baby carrots *(sweet, pungent)*

½ teaspoon ghee *(sweet)*

1 tablespoon Bragg's Liquid Aminos *(astringent, salty)*

1 teaspoon maple syrup *(sweet)*

1. Blanch the carrots by immersing in boiling water for 5 minutes. Remove and rinse immediately in cold water to stop the cooking and retain the color. Drain.
2. In a skillet, heat the ghee to the smoking point. Add the carrots and cook 3 minutes, until slightly browned. Add Bragg's Liquid Aminos and maple syrup. Toss and serve.

Serves 4 to 6

Prominent Tastes: *Sweet, Astringent*	
If you want to reduce	*eat*
VATA	SOME
PITTA	SOME
KAPHA	LESS

ℒEEKS AND ℒIMAS

◆

1 hour, 20 minutes to prepare

1 cup dried lima beans *(sweet, astringent)*

½ teaspoon salt *(salty)*

1 teaspoon olive oil *(sweet)*

2 large leeks, diced and well washed *(pungent, sweet)*

2 medium zucchini, diced *(sweet)*

6 roma tomatoes, diced *(sweet, sour)*

1 tablespoon Bragg's Liquid Aminos *(astringent, salty)*

1 tablespoon vegetable broth powder *(all)*

¼ teaspoon cardamom *(pungent, sweet)*

½ teaspoon cumin *(pungent)*

1. In a saucepan, bring 4 cups of water to a boil. Add the lima beans and salt and simmer for 1 hour.
2. In a large skillet, bring the oil to the smoking point. Sauté the leeks and zucchini for 5 minutes. Add the tomatoes and heat through.
3. Add the remaining ingredients and toss. Let stand 10 minutes before serving.

Serves 4 to 6

Prominent Tastes: *Sweet, Astringent*	
If you want to reduce	*eat*
VATA	SOME
PITTA	MORE
KAPHA	MORE

ℳɪɴᴛᴇᴅ ℘ᴇᴀ Sᴏᴜꜰꜰʟᴇ́

◆

Frozen peas can be used in winter,
but fresh peas are so aromatic and sweet!

40 minutes to prepare

½ teaspoon ghee *(sweet)*

2 medium shallots, chopped *(pungent)*

1 pound fresh peas *(sweet, astringent)*

2 eggs, beaten *(sweet)*

½ cup ricotta or Paneer cheese *(sweet)*

Pinch of tarragon *(pungent)*

2 teaspoons chopped fresh mint or 1 teaspoon dried *(pungent)*

Pinch of sea salt *(salty)*

2 tablespoons Bragg's Liquid Aminos *(astringent, salty)*

¼ cup fresh bread crumbs *(sweet)*

1. Preheat the oven to 350° F.
2. In a skillet, heat the ghee to the smoking point. Sauté the shallots until tender. Add the peas and continue to cook for 3 minutes. Process in a food processor until the peas and shallots are puréed.
3. Mix well with the eggs, ricotta or Paneer, tarragon, mint, salt, and Bragg's Liquid Aminos. Pour into an oiled casserole dish and sprinkle with the bread crumbs.
4. Bake for about 30 minutes, until firm and the bread crumbs are browned.

Serves 4 to 6

Prominent Taste: *Sweet*	
If you want to reduce	*eat*
VATA	MORE
PITTA	MORE
KAPHA	LESS

♥ Minted Rice and Peas

◆

Mint and peas are a harmonious blend.

20 minutes to prepare

1 cup basmati rice *(sweet)*
½ teaspoon sea salt *(salty)*
½ teaspoon ghee, optional *(sweet)*
1 cup cooked fresh or frozen
    organic peas *(sweet, astringent)*

1 tablespoon minced fresh mint or
    ½ tablespoon crushed dried mint
    (pungent)

1. In a saucepan, place the rice, 2½ cups of water, and salt. Bring to a boil and simmer about 15 minutes.
2. Add the remaining ingredients and toss gently.

Serves 4 to 6

Prominent Tastes: *Sweet, Astringent*	
If you want to reduce	eat
VATA	MORE
PITTA	MORE
KAPHA	LESS

♥ORANGE ALMOND RICE

◆

20 minutes to prepare

1 cup basmati rice *(sweet)*
Pinch of sea salt *(salty)*
1 tablespoon Bragg's Liquid
   Aminos *(astringent, salty)*
¼ cup orange juice concentrate
   (sweet, sour)

¼ teaspoon orange zest *(bitter)*
2 tablespoons ground or slivered
   toasted almonds *(sweet, bitter)*
Dash of grated nutmeg *(pungent)*

1. In a saucepan, bring 2 cups of water to a boil. Add the rice and salt and simmer 15 minutes.
2. Add Bragg's Liquid Aminos, orange juice concentrate, and orange zest. Toss.
3. Serve on plates, garnished with the almonds and nutmeg.

Serves 4 to 6

Prominent Tastes: *Sweet, Bitter*	
If you want to reduce	*eat*
VATA	MORE
PITTA	SOME
KAPHA	LESS

♥Orange Almond Spinach

◆

20 minutes to prepare

3 pounds spinach *(bitter)*
Pinch of sea salt *(salty)*
1 tablespoon Bragg's Liquid
 Aminos *(astringent, salty)*
¼ cup orange juice concentrate
 (sweet, sour)

¼ teaspoon orange zest *(bitter)*
2 tablespoons ground or slivered
 toasted almonds *(sweet, bitter)*
Dash of grated nutmeg *(pungent,
 astringent)*

1. In a skillet, bring 6 tablespoons of water to a boil. Add the spinach and salt to taste. Cook for 5 minutes, or until the spinach is just wilted. Don't overcook.
2. Add Bragg's Liquid Aminos, orange juice concentrate, and orange zest. Toss.
3. Serve on plates, garnished with the almonds and nutmeg.

Serves 4 to 6

Prominent Tastes: *Bitter, Sweet*	
If you want to reduce	*eat*
VATA	SOME
PITTA	SOME
KAPHA	MORE

Potato Hash

◆

The flesh of the Yellow Finn potato gives a buttery texture to this dish.

25 minutes to prepare

2 cups diced Yellow Finn potatoes *(astringent)*

1 cup diced leeks, washed well *(pungent, sweet)*

1 cup diced red pepper *(sweet, astringent)*

1 cup fresh corn kernels *(sweet)*

1 tablespoon olive oil *(sweet)*

1 teaspoon dried thyme *(pungent)*

½ teaspoon dried tarragon *(pungent)*

Dash of sea salt *(salty)*

Dash of pepper *(pungent)*

3 tablespoons chopped fresh cilantro *(pungent)*

1. Boil the potatoes in water to cover for 5 minutes. Drain well. Toss in a bowl with the rest of the ingredients.
2. Spray a skillet and sauté the potato mixture until browned and crispy. Serve immediately.

Serves 4 to 6

Prominent Tastes: *Pungent, Astringent*	
If you want to reduce	*eat*
VATA	LESS
PITTA	SOME
KAPHA	MORE

♥ QUINOA PILAF

◆

Quinoa is not actually a grain, although it is treated that way.
Its kissing cousin is the spinach plant!

20 minutes to prepare

1 cup quinoa *(sweet, astringent)*
½ teaspoon sea salt *(salty)*
1 tablespoon dried onion flakes
  (pungent, sweet)
1 tablespoon Bragg's Liquid
  Aminos *(astringent, salty)*

1 tablespoon vegetable broth
  powder *(all)*
½ teaspoon ghee, optional *(sweet)*

1. In a saucepan, bring 2 cups of water to a boil. Add the quinoa and salt and simmer for 15 minutes.
2. Add the onion flakes, Bragg's Liquid Aminos, vegetable broth powder, and the optional ghee. Let stand 5 minutes before serving.

Serves 4 to 6

Prominent Tastes: *Sweet, Astringent*	
If you want to reduce	*eat*
VATA	SOME
PITTA	MORE
KAPHA	SOME

Roasted Mustard Potatoes

◆

Serve this, warm or at room temperature, instead of potato salad.

1 hour to prepare

1 pound Yukon Gold or red
  potatoes, diced *(astringent)*
1 tablespoon olive oil *(sweet)*
1 tablespoon dried onion flakes
  (pungent, sweet)
Pinch of sea salt

1 tablespoon Bragg's Liquid
  Aminos *(astringent, salty)*
1 tablespoon Dijon mustard
  (pungent)
1 tablespoon honey, optional
  (sweet)

1. Preheat the oven to 400°F.
2. Toss the potatoes in the oil, onion flakes, salt, and Bragg's Liquid Aminos. Place in an oiled or sprayed baking dish. Cover with foil and roast for 30 to 40 minutes.
3. Remove the foil, toss, and continue roasting for an additional 15 minutes, until the potatoes are browned. Toss with the Dijon mustard. Honey may be added, if desired.

Serves 6 to 8

Prominent Tastes: *Astringent, Pungent*	
If you want to reduce	*eat*
VATA	LESS
PITTA	SOME
KAPHA	SOME

❤SAFFRON RICE

◆

This is great with curries or greens.

20 minutes to prepare

1 cup basmati rice *(sweet)*
½ teaspoon sea salt *(salty)*
⅛ teaspoon saffron threads
  (pungent)

1 teaspoon warm water
1 teaspoon ground cumin *(pungent)*

In a saucepan, place the rice, 2½ cups of water, and salt. While bringing to a boil, mix the saffron in the warm water and add to the rice with the cumin. Cook about 15 minutes.

Serves 4 to 6

Prominent Tastes: *Sweet, Pungent*	
If you want to reduce	*eat*
VATA	SOME
PITTA	SOME
KAPHA	LESS

Sweet Sweet Potatoes

◆

This is a favorite at The Center.
*Everyone loves it, although **Kaphas** should eat less.*

20 minutes to prepare

1 tablespoon ghee *(sweet)*

6 sweet potatoes, peeled and diced
  (sweet)

2 tablespoons Bragg's Liquid
  Aminos *(astringent, salty)*

2 tablespoons maple syrup *(sweet)*

2 tablespoons coconut *(sweet)*

1 teaspoon cumin *(pungent)*

1. In a large skillet, heat the ghee to the smoking point. Sauté the sweet potatoes until tender and browned, about 10 minutes, stirring frequently with a spatula.
2. Remove from heat, toss with the remaining ingredients, and serve warm.

Serves 6 to 8

Prominent Taste: *Sweet*	
If you want to reduce	*eat*
VATA	MORE
PITTA	MORE
KAPHA	LESS

BREAD

◆

Bread is the all-time comfort food. Everyone loves bread, in all its shapes, sizes, and guises. The variety of breads is unlimited and includes yeasted breads, flatbread, chappatis, focaccia, pizza dough, muffins, and quick breads. In every culture, some form of bread goes with the meal.

With the advent of bread machines, much of the meditative quality of mixing and kneading bread is lost. The human touch through loving hands contributes wholeness and nourishment to the bread, and brings personal satisfaction to the baker.

Allow yourself time to enjoy the experience of kneading bread, dusting your hands with flour, shaping the loaves, and watching them rise in warm places. Your friends and family will appreciate your effort when they are greeted by the aromas of the warm, crusty loaves you pull from the oven.

Some dietary systems recommend avoiding all white bread, but when scattered throughout your week of menus with whole wheat or other whole grain recipes, white bread offers satisfaction to your palate and comfort to your soul. We recommend baking your white bread with organic unbleached flour, and wheat breads with organic whole wheat pastry flour and other whole ingredients. Vary the breads throughout the week just as you vary your vegetables and grains.

ANADAMA BREAD

CINNAMON RAISIN
BREAD

FOCACCIA

DARK DATE NUT BREAD

FOUGASSE

FRENCH BREAD

GINGER-MOLASSES
MUFFINS

OATMEAL MUFFINS

GOODY MUFFINS

ITALIANATE MUFFINS

NAAN

PITA BREAD

SPELT BREAD

WHOLE WHEAT
CHAPPATIS

ANADAMA BREAD

◆

This early-American favorite uses whole grain flour and cornmeal for a rich, hearty flavor. Serve with Vegetable Barley Casserole (page 97) for a warm, wholesome lunch.

2 hours to prepare

1 tablespoon active dry yeast
1 cup lukewarm water
1 tablespoon soft butter, ghee, or oil *(sweet)*
¼ cup dark molasses *(sweet)*
½ cup cornmeal *(sweet)*

½ teaspoon sea salt *(salty)*
1 cup organic unbleached white flour *(sweet, astringent)*
2 cups organic whole wheat flour *(sweet, astringent)*

1. In a large bowl, dissolve the yeast in the water. Add the butter, ghee, or oil with the molasses and cornmeal; stir to dissolve. Add the salt and flour, adding more flour if necessary, until the dough comes away from the sides of bowl as you mix. Knead in the bowl for about 5 minutes.
2. Cover and let rise until double, about an hour. Set near a warm stove or oven to quicken the rising process. Roll the dough out onto a floured surface. Punch down with your hand and divide into 2 equal-sized balls. Set aside for 10 minutes.
3. Preheat the oven to 375° F.
4. Place the loaves into lightly oiled or sprayed 9-inch bread pans and let rise again until double. Brush with water and make a cut down the middle of the loaves with a sharp knife. Place on the middle rack of the oven over a steaming pan of hot water, which you have placed on the bottom of the oven. The loaves are done when you hear a hollow sound when tapping lightly with your finger, 40 to 50 minutes. Cool on racks.

Makes 2 loaves

Prominent Taste: *Sweet*	
If you want to reduce	*eat*
VATA	SOME
PITTA	SOME
KAPHA	LESS

♥CINNAMON RAISIN BREAD

♦

Most recipes for cinnamon raisin bread use melted butter for adhering the filling to the insides of the dough. Here we use water for a nonfat bread treat.

2 to 4 hours to prepare

2 tablespoons active dry yeast

2 tablespoons turbinado sugar *(sweet)*

2 cups lukewarm water

⅔ cup nonfat dry milk *(sweet)*

5 to 7 cups sifted organic unbleached white flour or a mixture of white and whole wheat pastry flour *(sweet, astringent)*

½ tablespoon sea salt *(salty)*

Filling

¼ cup lukewarm water

1 cup raisins or currants *(sweet)*

2 tablespoons cinnamon *(pungent, bitter)*

1 tablespoon cardamom *(pungent, sweet)*

1. In a large bowl, dissolve the yeast and sugar in the water and let stand for 10 minutes. Stir in the nonfat dry milk, flour, and salt. Knead in the bowl for about 5 minutes. Cover and let rise until double, 1 to 2 hours. Set it near a warm stove or oven to quicken the rising process.

2. Roll out onto a floured surface. Punch down with your hand and divide into 2 equal pieces.

3. Preheat the oven to 375° F.

4. Dust the rolling surface with flour and roll out each piece into a 6 × 12-inch rectangle. Brush with the water, then sprinkle with the raisins, cinnamon, and cardamom. Carefully roll up, shaping into jelly rolls.

5. Place the loaves, seam sides down, in 2 lightly oiled or sprayed 9-inch bread pans. Cover with a towel and let stand until the loaves rise above the top of the pans, 30 to 40 minutes.

6. Place a pan of hot water on the bottom of the oven. Place the pans on the middle rack and bake for 35 to 40 minutes, or until the loaves are golden brown. Cool on racks.

Makes 2 loaves

Prominent Taste: *Sweet*	
If you want to reduce	*eat*
VATA	MORE
PITTA	SOME
KAPHA	LESS

$\mathcal{F}$OCACCIA

◆

Much like pizza dough, this Italian favorite can be plain or generously covered with toppings.

2 hours to prepare

2 tablespoons active dry yeast

2 cups lukewarm water

⅛ cup plus 2 tablespoons olive oil *(sweet)*

5 to 7 cups organic unbleached white flour or organic whole wheat pastry flour *(sweet, astringent)*

½ teaspoon sea salt *(salty)*

Topping possibilities: Olive oil, dry onion flakes, coarse sea salt, caramelized red onion, rosemary, oregano

1. In a large bowl, dissolve the yeast in the lukewarm water. Add the oil, 5 cups of flour, and the salt. Mix until the dough comes away from the sides of the bowl, adding a little more flour, if necessary.
2. Dust the kneading surface with flour. Turn out the dough and knead for 8 to 10 minutes, or until smooth and elastic.
3. Transfer to a large oiled bowl and let rise until doubled, 40 to 70 minutes. Punch the dough down and turn out onto a floured surface. Cut into 2 equal pieces and let stand for 15 minutes.
4. Preheat the oven to 400°F.
5. Oil or spray two 9 × 12-inch baking sheets. Place each piece on a baking sheet and, pressing out and away with the palms of your hands, cover the pan with the dough. At this point, the focaccia dough can be brushed with oil, sprinkled or spread with the desired topping, or left plain. Cover and let rise 25 minutes.
6. Place a pan of hot water in the bottom of the oven. Bake the focaccia on the middle rack for 10 to 15 minutes, or until golden brown. Serve warm.

Makes 2 loaves

Prominent Taste: *Sweet*	
If you want to reduce	*eat*
VATA	SOME
PITTA	SOME
KAPHA	LESS

Dark Date Nut Bread

◆

*Baked in 1-pound coffee cans, these dark, moist loaves are
beautiful hostess presents or holiday gifts.*

1½ hours to prepare

½ cup boiling water

½ cup currants *(sweet)*

½ cup chopped date pieces *(sweet)*

1 teaspoon unsalted butter or ghee
(sweet)

¾ teaspoon baking soda *(salty)*

¼ cup dark molasses *(sweet)*

1 cup organic unbleached white
flour or whole wheat pastry flour
(sweet, astringent)

⅛ teaspoon sea salt *(salty)*

1 egg *(sweet)*

½ teaspoon vanilla extract *(sweet)*

¼ cup chopped walnuts, optional
(sweet)

1. Preheat the oven to 350°F.
2. In a bowl, pour the boiling water over the currants, dates, butter or
   ghee, and baking soda. Mix in the molasses. In a separate bowl, mix the
   flour and salt together; blend with the fruit mixture and the remaining
   ingredients.
3. Pour into an oiled 1-pound coffee can or 1-pound bread pan and bake
   for 1 hour, until crust forms. Remove from the pan to cool.

Makes 1 loaf

Prominent Taste: *Sweet*	
If you want to reduce	*eat*
VATA	MORE
PITTA	SOME
KAPHA	LESS

Fougasse

◆

These crusty flatbreads are great snacks or appetizers, or they can accompany any meal. Make the sponge the night before you wish to serve this yummy stuff. Make lots!

2 to 3 hours to prepare

Sponge

1 tablespoon active dry yeast
½ cup lukewarm water
1 cup organic unbleached white flour or organic whole wheat pastry flour *(sweet, astringent)*

1 tablespoon active dry yeast
1 cup lukewarm water

2 tablespoons olive oil *(sweet)*
3 to 5 cups organic unbleached white flour or organic whole wheat pastry flour *(sweet, astringent)*
½ teaspoon sea salt *(salty)*
1 cup cornmeal, for dusting pans *(sweet)*

1. Make the sponge: Dissolve the yeast in the lukewarm water. Add the flour and mix well. Cover and let stand overnight.
2. Using a wooden spoon, stir the sponge. Dissolve the yeast in the lukewarm water and add to the sponge with the oil, 3 cups of flour, and salt. Mix until the dough comes away from the sides of the bowl, adding a little more flour, if necessary.
3. Dust the kneading surface with flour. Turn out the dough and knead for 8 to 10 minutes, or until smooth and elastic. Transfer to a large oiled bowl and let rise until doubled, 1 to 2 hours.
4. Punch down and turn out onto a floured surface. Cut into 8 equal pieces and shape each piece into rounds. Let stand for 15 minutes.
5. Preheat the oven to 400° F.
6. Roll or stretch the rounds into ovals or triangles and place on baking sheets that have been dusted with cornmeal. Cover and let rise until doubled in size. Press with your thumbs in several places to create a textured surface and make several slashes with a sharp knife.

7. Place a pan of hot water in the bottom of the oven. Bake the fougasse on the middle rack for 10 to 15 minutes, or until golden brown. Serve warm.

Makes 8 pieces

Prominent Taste: *Sweet*	
If you want to reduce	*eat*
VATA	SOME
PITTA	SOME
KAPHA	LESS

♥ℱRENCH ℬREAD

◆

This bread is easy, great, warm—wow!

2 to 3 hours to prepare

2 tablespoons active dry yeast
2 tablespoons turbinado sugar
  (sweet)
4 cups lukewarm water

8 cups sifted organic unbleached white flour or a mixture of white and whole wheat pastry flour *(sweet, astringent)*
1 teaspoon sea salt *(salty)*

1. In a large bowl, dissolve the yeast and sugar in 2 cups of the water. Let stand for 10 minutes. Stir in the flour and salt. Add just enough of the rest of the water to hold the dough together; it will form a soft, sticky dough.
2. Knead in the bowl for about 5 minutes, adding more flour, if necessary, to keep it from being too sticky. Cover and let rise until double, 1 to 2 hours. Set near a warm stove or oven to quicken the rising process.

3. Preheat the oven to 400°F.

4. When the dough has risen, punch it down with your hand and divide into loaves: 2 medium loaf pans, or 1 large one. Clay will produce the best crust. Let rise again for 25 minutes, or until risen over the top of the pans.

5. Bake for 40 minutes on the middle rack over pans of hot water placed on the bottom of the oven, until browned and crusty.

Makes 1 large or 2 medium loaves

Prominent Taste: *Sweet*	
If you want to reduce	*eat*
VATA	SOME
PITTA	SOME
KAPHA	LESS

VARIATION: Add Italian herbs to the dry flour for an Italianate flavor.

Ginger-Molasses Muffins

◆

Using fresh ginger gives these treats a pungent quality.
Serve them for breakfast with Paneer cheese and a warm
cup of chai, or for dessert after a special curry luncheon.

30 minutes to prepare

¼ cup butter or ghee, at room temperature *(sweet)*

½ cup dark molasses *(sweet)*

2 large eggs *(sweet)*

2½ cups organic unbleached white flour or whole wheat pastry flour *(sweet, astringent)*

1 teaspoon baking soda *(salty)*

¼ teaspoon sea salt *(salty)*

1 teaspoon cinnamon *(pungent, bitter)*

2-inch piece of fresh ginger, grated or finely chopped *(pungent, sweet)*

¼ teaspoon allspice *(pungent)*

¼ teaspoon cardamom *(pungent, sweet)*

1 cup boiling water

1. Preheat the oven to 375° F.
2. In a bowl, mix together the butter or ghee, molasses, and eggs until smooth. Blend in the remaining ingredients gently.
3. Pour the batter into lightly oiled or sprayed muffin cups. Bake 20 minutes. Cool on racks.

Makes 12 muffins

Prominent Tastes: *Sweet, Pungent*	
If you want to reduce	*eat*
VATA	MORE
PITTA	LESS
KAPHA	SOME

OATMEAL MUFFINS

◆

40 minutes to prepare

3 cups organic unbleached white flour *(sweet, astringent)*

2 cups oats *(sweet)*

2 teaspoons baking powder *(salty)*

1 teaspoon baking soda *(salty)*

1 teaspoon sea salt *(salty)*

½ cup turbinado sugar *(sweet)*

2 tablespoons cinnamon *(pungent, bitter)*

¼ cup maple syrup *(sweet)*

2 cups plain nonfat yogurt *(sweet, sour)*

2 eggs *(sweet)*

½ cup nonfat milk *(sweet)*

3 tablespoons ghee *(sweet)*

1. Preheat the oven to 400° F.
2. In a large bowl, sift together the dry ingredients. Combine with the remaining ingredients and blend gently.
3. Pour into 2 sprayed or oiled muffin tins. Bake for 25 minutes.

Makes 24 muffins

Prominent Taste: *Sweet*	
If you want to reduce	*eat*
VATA	MORE
PITTA	LESS
KAPHA	LESS

Goody Muffins

◆

These power-packed muffins start your day with a bang.
They contain all six tastes!

30 minutes to prepare

¼ cup organic unbleached white flour *(sweet, astringent)*

1½ cups whole wheat pastry flour *(sweet, astringent)*

¼ cup bran flakes *(sweet, astringent)*

¼ cup oat bran *(sweet)*

¼ cup wheat germ *(sweet, astringent)*

¼ cup ground sunflower seeds *(sweet, bitter)*

¼ cup ground pine nuts *(sweet)*

¼ cup nonfat dry milk *(sweet)*

1 tablespoon baking powder *(salty)*

¼ teaspoon sea salt *(salty)*

2 eggs *(sweet)*

1 cup plain nonfat yogurt *(sweet, sour)*

¼ cup canola *(sweet)* or sunflower *(sweet)* oil for **Pitta** and **Kapha** or safflower oil *(sweet, pungent)* for **Vata**

½ cup turbinado sugar *(sweet)*

¼ cup each:

chopped date pieces *(sweet)*

apricots *(sweet, sour)*

raisins or currants *(sweet)* (good for **Kapha,** leave out for **Vata**)

coconut *(sweet)*

1. Preheat the oven to 400° F.
2. In a large bowl, combine the first 10 ingredients.
3. In a separate mixing bowl, blend the eggs, yogurt, oil, and sugar gently. Add the fruit and coconut. Fold in the other ingredients.
4. Pour the batter into lightly oiled or sprayed muffins cups. Bake 15 to 20 minutes. Cool on racks and serve warm or at room temperature.

Makes 12 muffins

Prominent Tastes: *All*	
If you want to reduce	*eat*
VATA	SOME
PITTA	SOME
KAPHA	SOME

$\mathcal{I}$TALIANATE $\mathcal{M}$UFFINS

◆

These savory muffins are great with pasta or as an accompaniment to salad.
*For **Vatas** and **Pittas**, cheese may be added.*

30 minutes to prepare

2 cups organic unbleached white flour *(sweet, astringent)*
1 tablespoon baking powder *(salty)*
½ teaspoon sea salt *(salty)*
¼ teaspoon dried oregano *(pungent)*
¼ teaspoon dried crumbled rosemary *(pungent, bitter)*
¼ teaspoon dried thyme *(pungent)*
⅛ teaspoon chili flakes *(pungent)*
2 eggs *(sweet)*

1 cup nonfat milk *(sweet)*
¼ cup olive oil *(sweet)*
1 tablespoon turbinado sugar *(sweet)*
1 garlic clove, minced *(all but sour)*
¼ cup sun-dried tomatoes, drained and chopped *(sweet, sour)*
1 cup grated Parmesan cheese, optional *(sweet)*

1. Preheat the oven to 400° F.
2. In a large bowl, combine the first 7 ingredients.
3. In a separate mixing bowl, gently blend the eggs, milk, oil, and sugar together. Add the garlic and sun-dried tomatoes. Fold in the other ingredients.

4. Pour the batter into lightly oiled or sprayed muffins cups. Bake 15 to 20 minutes. Cool on racks and serve warm or at room temperature.

Makes 12 muffins

Prominent Tastes: *All*	
If you want to reduce	*eat*
VATA	SOME
PITTA	SOME
KAPHA	SOME

❤ 𝒩AAN

◆

Don't have a tandoor oven in your backyard that reaches 700° F.? That's okay. A temperature of 500° F. in your home oven will work. Naan is the Northern Indian equivalent to pita, lavash, and fougasse.

40 to 50 minutes to prepare

1 tablespoon active dry yeast
½ cup lukewarm water
1 cup plain nonfat yogurt *(sweet, sour)*
2 tablespoons vegetable oil *(sweet)*

3 to 5 cups organic unbleached white flour or organic whole wheat pastry flour *(sweet, astringent)*
½ teaspoon sea salt *(salty)*

1. In a large bowl, dissolve the yeast in the lukewarm water. Add the yogurt, oil, 3 cups of flour, and the salt. Mix until the dough comes away from the sides of the bowl, adding a little more flour, if necessary. Don't add too much, though; this dough should be on the soft side.
2. Dust the kneading surface with flour. Turn out the dough and knead for 8 to 10 minutes, or until smooth and elastic. Transfer to a large oiled bowl and let rise until doubled, 30 to 40 minutes.
3. Punch the dough down and turn out onto a floured surface. Cut into 12 equal pieces and shape each piece into rounds. Let stand for 15 minutes.
4. Preheat the oven to 500° F.
5. Roll or stretch the rounds into 6-inch circles. Place a large baking sheet in the oven for 15 minutes. Open the oven door and quickly place the dough rounds, 2 at a time, onto the hot baking sheet. Bake 1 to 2 minutes on each side, until golden brown in places.
6. Cover the completed naans with a towel while baking others. These are best served warm; however, they can be cooled and refrigerated in plastic bags.

Makes 12 pieces

Prominent Taste: *Sweet*	
If you want to reduce	*eat*
VATA	SOME
PITTA	SOME
KAPHA	LESS

$\mathcal{P}$ITA $\mathcal{B}$READ

◆

1½ hours to prepare

1 tablespoon active dry yeast
1 teaspoon turbinado sugar *(sweet)*
1¼ cups lukewarm water
2 tablespoons olive oil *(sweet)*

1 teaspoon sea salt *(salty)*
3 cups sifted organic unbleached
white flour plus more, for rolling
(sweet, astringent)

1. In a large bowl, stir the yeast, sugar, and half the water together. Let stand about 10 minutes, until bubbly. Add the remaining water, oil, salt, and half the flour. Stir with a wooden spoon until blended. Add enough of the remaining flour, a little at a time, until the dough is no longer sticky.
2. Preheat the oven to 500° F.
3. Turn the dough onto a floured board and cut into 6 equal pieces. Pat each into a ¼-inch-thick circle. Cover with a towel and let rest 30 minutes, until slightly puffed. Gather the balls into your hands one at a time and squeeze out the air. Roll into ¼-inch-thick circles again.
4. Lay the circles 1 inch apart on an ungreased baking sheet and bake on the lowest oven rack for 5 minutes. Move to a higher rack and bake an additional 2 minutes, until the circles are puffy and browned. Cool. Store in a plastic bag.

Makes 6 pitas

Prominent Taste: *Sweet*	
If you want to reduce	*eat*
VATA	MORE
PITTA	MORE
KAPHA	LESS

♥SPELT BREAD

❖

Spelt, an ancient whole grain,
is often used for those with a wheat intolerance.

2 to 3 hours to prepare

2 tablespoons active dry yeast
2 tablespoons turbinado sugar
 (sweet)
4 cups lukewarm water

8 cups organic whole spelt flour
 (sweet, astringent)
½ tablespoon sea salt *(salty)*

1. In a large bowl, dissolve the yeast and sugar in 2 cups of the water. Let stand for 10 minutes.
2. Stir in the flour and salt. Add just enough of the rest of the water to hold the dough together; it will form a soft, sticky dough. Knead in the bowl for about 5 minutes.
3. Cover and let rise until double, 1 to 2 hours. Set near a warm stove or oven to quicken the rising process.
4. Preheat the oven to 400° F.
5. When the dough has risen, punch it down with your hand and divide into loaves: 2 medium loaf pans or 1 large one. Clay will produce the best crust. Let rise again for 25 minutes, or until risen over the top of the pans.
6. Bake for about 40 minutes, or until browned and crusty.

Makes 2 medium loaves or 1 large loaf

Prominent Taste: *Sweet*	
If you want to reduce	*eat*
VATA	MORE
PITTA	MORE
KAPHA	SOME

Whole Wheat Chappatis

◆

This is a good yeastless bread.

1½ hours to prepare

2¼ cups whole wheat pastry flour plus extra, for rolling *(sweet, astringent)*

2 teaspoons sunflower or canola oil *(sweet)*

Pinch of sea salt *(salty)*

1¼ cups lukewarm water

1. With a wooden spoon, mix the flour, oil, and salt in a large bowl. Add the water and mix into a soft dough. Cover and let stand for 1 hour.
2. Moisten your hands with oil and make 25 to 30 small balls. Roll the balls in a small bowl of flour. Using a rolling pin, roll out on a floured surface to form 6-inch circles.
3. To cook chappatis, heat a large skillet or griddle to medium. Cook each chappati ½ minute on the first side, about 1 minute on the second side, until it puffs. Serve immediately or keep covered until ready to use.

Makes 25 to 30 chappatis

Prominent Taste: *Sweet*	
If you want to reduce	*eat*
VATA	MORE
PITTA	MORE
KAPHA	LESS

$\mathcal{D}$ ESSERTS

◆

Ancient seers knew that part of the glory of life was its sweetness. We think it's good to metabolize some sweetness every day.

Many of our desserts are low in fat, but some are not. Use your good judgment in the amount of dessert you eat and how often you eat it. Concentrated sweetness is best consumed at midday, when the digestive fire is strongest.

APRICOT BARS

BAKED APPLES

BAKLAVA

CHOCOLATE CHIP
COOKIES

DATE BARS

FRESH BLUEBERRY CAKE

FRENCH APPLE CAKE

GLAZED PEAR TART OR
POACHED PEARS

GINGER-MOLASSES
COOKIES

GRANOLA BARS

LEMON BARS

OUTRAGEOUS OATMEAL
COOKIES

PRUNE CAKE

Apricot Bars

◆

This recipe is good for all body types.

40 minutes to prepare

<u>Crust</u> | <u>Topping</u>

2 cups organic unbleached white flour *(sweet, astringent)*

4 tablespoons turbinado sugar *(sweet)*

¼ cup (½ stick) cold unsalted butter *(sweet)*

½ cup organic unbleached white flour *(sweet, astringent)*

½ cup turbinado sugar *(sweet)*

1 teaspoon baking powder *(salty)*

1 teaspoon sea salt *(salty)*

2 eggs *(sweet)*

2 teaspoons vanilla extract *(sweet)*

2 cups chopped dried apricots *(sweet, sour)*

1. Preheat the oven to 350°F.
2. Make the crust: In a food processor, mix the flour and sugar. Cut the cold butter into pieces and process with the flour and sugar until mealy. Press into the bottom of a 9 × 13-inch baking pan and bake 15 minutes.
3. Prepare the topping: In a small bowl, sift the flour, sugar, baking powder, and salt. Add the remaining ingredients and stir until well mixed.
4. After cooling the crumb mixture, spread the topping over it and bake 20 minutes. Cool, cut into bars, and serve warm or at room temperature.

Makes 12 to 18 bars

Prominent Taste: *Sweet*	
If you want to reduce	eat
VATA	SOME
PITTA	SOME
KAPHA	LESS

♥ℬAKED ℭPPLES

◆

Baked apples make a delicious breakfast or dessert.

45 minutes to prepare

2 Pippin or Granny Smith apples
  (sweet, astringent)
½ teaspoon ghee *(sweet)*
2 teaspoons ground pine nuts
  (sweet)

1 teaspoon cinnamon *(pungent)*
1 teaspoon maple syrup *(sweet)*
¼ teaspoon ground ginger
  (pungent)
¼ cup apple juice *(sweet, astringent)*

1. Preheat the oven to 400° F.
2. Peel the top of the apples about ⅓ of the way down. Cut out a 1-inch piece of the center cores.
3. Mix the ghee, nuts, cinnamon, maple syrup, and ginger together and put in the well in the center of the apples. Place in a baking dish with the apple juice, cover with foil, and bake about 30 minutes. Uncover, baste with apple juice, and bake until soft, about 15 more minutes.

Serves 2

Prominent Tastes: *Sweet, Astringent*	
If you want to reduce	*eat*
VATA	SOME
PITTA	SOME
KAPHA	SOME

ℬAKLAVA

◆

Made with maple syrup instead of honey, these goodies are awesome.

1 hour to prepare

1 cup sunflower seeds *(sweet, bitter)*
½ cup pine nuts *(sweet)*
½ cup roasted or blanched almonds *(sweet, bitter)*
1 cup raisins or currants *(sweet)*
½ cup shredded coconut *(sweet)*
¼ cup maple syrup *(sweet)*

1 teaspoon vanilla extract *(sweet)*
Filo sheets *(sweet)*
Soft or melted ghee, for brushing *(sweet)*
Sesame seeds *(sweet)*
Maple syrup *(sweet)*

1. Preheat the oven to 350° F.
2. In a food processor, combine the first 7 ingredients. Process for about 30 seconds, just long enough to chop up the ingredients but not so long as to pulverize them.
3. Spread the ghee over 4 sheets of the filo, stacking as you go. Remember, the more ghee you use, the more calories from fat are added. Just use barely enough to hold the filo sheets together.
4. Place the filling at one edge of the filo stack and roll up. Brush roll lightly with the ghee.
5. Cut into small squares and place on a cookie sheet. Sprinkle with sesame seeds and bake for about 25 minutes, or until golden. Drizzle with maple syrup. Cool completely before serving.

Makes 24 to 30 pieces

Prominent Taste: *Sweet*	
If you want to reduce	*eat*
VATA	MORE
PITTA	MORE
KAPHA	LESS

CHOCOLATE CHIP COOKIES

◆

Chocolate is not described in classic Ayurvedic texts, as it was not grown in India. Some scientists believe it has chemicals that mimic those produced by people in love.

1 hour to prepare

1 cup turbinado sugar *(sweet)*

¾ cup (1½ sticks) butter, melted *(sweet)*

2 eggs *(sweet)*

1 tablespoon vanilla extract *(sweet)*

2¼ cups organic unbleached white flour or whole wheat pastry flour *(sweet, astringent)*

1 teaspoon baking soda *(salty)*

¼ teaspoon sea salt *(salty)*

2 cups chocolate chips *(pungent, bitter)*

½ cup ground nuts of your choice, optional *(sweet, bitter)*

1. Preheat the oven to 375° F.
2. In a bowl, blend the first 4 ingredients. Add the flour, baking soda, and salt and mix well.
3. Fold in the chocolate chips and add nuts, if desired.
4. Drop by teaspoonfuls onto an oiled or sprayed baking sheet and bake for 8 to 10 minutes, until browned on the bottom but still soft in the middle. *Don't overcook. The cookies should be browned on the bottom only.*

Makes 60 cookies

Prominent Taste: *Sweet*	
If you want to reduce	eat
VATA	SOME
PITTA	SOME
KAPHA	LESS

$\mathcal{D}$ATE $\mathcal{B}$ARS

◆

40 minutes to prepare

<table>
<tr><td><u>Crust</u></td><td><u>Topping</u></td></tr>
<tr><td>

2 cups flour *(sweet, astringent)*
4 tablespoons turbinado sugar *(sweet)*
¼ cup (½ stick) cold unsalted butter *(sweet)*

</td><td>

½ cup flour *(sweet, astringent)*
½ cup turbinado sugar *(sweet)*
1 teaspoon baking powder *(salty)*
1 teaspoon sea salt *(salty)*
2 eggs *(sweet)*
2 teaspoons vanilla extract *(sweet)*
1 cup coconut *(sweet)*
2 cups chopped dates *(sweet)*
1 cup chopped pine nuts *(sweet)*

</td></tr>
</table>

1. Preheat the oven to 350° F.
2. Make the crust: In a food processor, mix the flour and sugar. Cut the cold butter into pieces and mix with the flour and sugar until mealy. Press into the bottom of a 9 × 13-inch baking pan and bake 15 minutes.
3. Make the topping: Sift the flour, sugar, baking powder, and salt into a bowl. Add the remaining ingredients and stir until well mixed.
4. After cooling the crumb mixture, spread the topping over it and bake 20 minutes. Cool, cut into bars, and serve warm or at room temperature.

Makes 12 to 18 bars

Prominent Taste: *Sweet*	
If you want to reduce	*eat*
VATA	SOME
PITTA	SOME
KAPHA	LESS

ℱRESH ℬLUEBERRY ℂAKE

◆

1½ hours to prepare

Cake

2 pounds fresh blueberries *(sweet, astringent)*

2 teaspoons cinnamon *(pungent, bitter)*

1 teaspoon nutmeg *(pungent, astringent)*

2 cups organic unbleached white flour *(sweet, astringent)*

2 teaspoons baking powder *(salty)*

½ cup turbinado sugar *(sweet)*

¼ cup nonfat milk *(sweet)*

¼ cup ghee *(sweet)*

4 eggs *(sweet)*

Topping

2 eggs *(sweet)*

¼ cup ghee *(sweet)*

1 cup turbinado sugar *(sweet)*

2 teaspoons vanilla extract *(sweet)*

1. Preheat the oven to 325° F. Spray or oil a 9 × 12-inch cake pan.
2. In a large bowl, toss the blueberries with the cinnamon and nutmeg; place in the cake pan. Put all the remaining cake ingredients in a bowl and beat well. Carefully pour the batter over the blueberries. Bake for about 45 minutes, or until golden brown.
3. Cream together the topping ingredients. Remove the cake from the oven, spoon the topping over it, and return the cake to the oven for about 20 minutes, until the topping is browned and bubbly.

Makes 12 to 18 pieces

Prominent Tastes: *Sweet, Astringent*	
If you want to reduce	eat
VATA	SOME
PITTA	SOME
KAPHA	LESS

French Apple Cake

◆

*Cooked apples decrease **Vata**.*
This dessert goes well with a warm cup of chai.

1½ hours to prepare

Cake

2 pounds Granny Smith or Pippin apples, cored and chopped *(sweet, astringent)*

2 teaspoons cinnamon *(pungent, bitter)*

1 teaspoon nutmeg *(pungent, astringent)*

2 cups organic unbleached white flour *(sweet, astringent)*

2 teaspoons baking powder *(salty)*

½ cup turbinado sugar *(sweet)*

¼ cup nonfat milk *(sweet)*

¼ cup ghee *(sweet)*

4 eggs *(sweet)*

Topping

2 eggs *(sweet)*

¼ cup ghee *(sweet)*

1 cup turbinado sugar *(sweet)*

2 teaspoons vanilla extract *(sweet)*

1. Preheat the oven to 325°F. Spray or oil a 9 × 12-inch cake pan.
2. In a large bowl, toss the chopped apples with the cinnamon and nutmeg and place in the cake pan. Put all the remaining cake ingredients in a bowl and beat well. Pour the batter over the apples and bake for about 45 minutes, or until golden brown.
3. Cream together the topping ingredients. Remove the cake from the oven, spoon the topping over it, and return the cake to the oven for about 20 minutes, until the topping is browned and bubbly.

Makes 12 to 18 pieces

Prominent Tastes: *Sweet, Astringent*	
If you want to reduce	*eat*
VATA	SOME
PITTA	SOME
KAPHA	SOME

GLAZED PEAR TART OR ♥POACHED PEARS

❖

When poached in grape juice, the pears turn a rich purple.
*This is pacifying to **Vata** and **Pitta**.*

1½ hours to prepare tart
45 minutes to prepare poached pairs

7 almost ripe Bartlett pears *(sweet)*

1 quart grape juice *(sweet, sour)*

1 tablespoon crystallized ginger *(pungent, sweet)*

1 teaspoon cinnamon *(pungent, bitter)*

1 tablespoon unsalted butter *(sweet)*

⅛ cup turbinado sugar *(sweet)*

1 sheet Pepperidge Farm Frozen Puff Pastry *(sweet)*

1 cup boysenberry jam *(sweet, sour)*

1. Preheat the oven to 400° F.
2. Poach the pears in the grape juice and spices for 25 to 35 minutes, until cooked but still firm. Remove from the pot and drain well.
3. Reduce the juice to a syrup. Add the butter and sugar.* Cool.
4. Cut the pears in half lengthwise.

*Stop at this point for Poached Pears, spooning the syrup over the pears to serve.

5. Roll out the pastry dough according to package directions to fit into a baking sheet. Crimp the edges. Bake for 25 minutes or until golden. Cool. Spread with the boysenberry jam. Arrange the pears, cut side down, on the pastry and pour the thickened syrup over the pears. Serve promptly.

Makes 10 to 12 pieces
Makes 7 pears

Prominent Taste: *Sweet*	
If you want to reduce	*eat*
VATA	MORE
PITTA	MORE
KAPHA	LESS

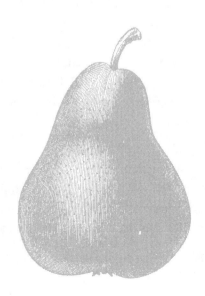

GINGER-MOLASSES COOKIES

◆

1½ hours to prepare

¾ cup turbinado sugar plus more, for rolling *(sweet)*

½ cup ghee *(sweet)*

1 egg *(sweet)*

½ cup molasses *(sweet)*

2 teaspoons ground ginger *(pungent, sweet)*

1 teaspoon ground cinnamon *(pungent, bitter)*

2 teaspoons baking soda *(salty)*

½ teaspoon sea salt *(salty)*

2¾ cups organic unbleached white flour *(sweet, astringent)*

1. Preheat the oven to 325°F.
2. In a bowl, blend ¾ cup sugar and the ghee well with a wooden spoon. Add the egg and molasses and mix well. Add the remaining ingredients and mix well. The mixture should be soft. Dust lightly with flour, wrap in plastic, and refrigerate for 30 minutes.
3. Shape into teaspoon-size balls and roll in the sugar. Place 1 inch apart on an oiled or sprayed cookie sheet, pressing flat with 2 fingers. Bake for about 10 minutes, or just until cracks appear on top. *The cookies should be browned on the bottom only.* Cool on a wire rack.

Makes 36 cookies

Prominent Tastes: *Sweet, Pungent*	
If you want to reduce	*eat*
VATA	SOME
PITTA	SOME
KAPHA	SOME

GRANOLA BARS

◆

This is a good breakfast item or snack.

40 minutes to prepare

¼ cup turbinado sugar *(sweet)*
½ cup (1 stick) unsalted butter,
melted *(sweet)*
2 eggs *(sweet)*
1 tablespoon vanilla extract *(sweet)*
1 cup organic unbleached white
flour *(sweet, astringent)*

1 teaspoon baking soda *(salty)*
¼ teaspoon sea salt *(salty)*
2 cups Granola (page 174) *(sweet)*
¼ cup currants or raisins *(sweet)*

1. Preheat the oven to 375° F.
2. Blend the first 4 ingredients. Add the flour, baking soda, and salt and mix well. Fold in the Granola and currants or raisins.
3. Press into an oiled or sprayed 9 × 12-inch baking dish. Bake for 10 to 15 minutes, until lightly brown but still soft in the middle. *Don't overcook.*

Makes 12 to 18 bars

Prominent Taste: *Sweet*	
If you want to reduce	*eat*
VATA	SOME
PITTA	SOME
KAPHA	LESS

ℒEMON ℬARS

◆

These are rich, but everyone wants this recipe.

45 minutes to prepare

Crust

2 cups organic unbleached white
  flour *(sweet, astringent)*
¼ cup turbinado sugar *(sweet)*
1 cup (2 sticks) cold unsalted butter
  (sweet)

Topping

3 eggs *(sweet)*
½ cup (1 stick) unsalted butter,
  melted *(sweet)*
1 cup turbinado sugar *(sweet)*
½ cup lemon juice *(sour, astringent)*

Confectioners' sugar, for sprinkling,
  optional *(sweet)*

1. Preheat the oven to 350° F.
2. Make the crust: In a food processor, mix the flour and sugar. Cut the cold butter into pieces and process with the flour and sugar until mealy. Press into the bottom of a 9 × 13-inch baking pan. Bake 15 minutes. Cool slightly.
3. In a food processor, combine the topping ingredients and process for 45 seconds. Pour evenly over the pastry.
4. Bake 25 minutes until set. Do not brown. Cool completely. Cut into small squares. Sprinkle with confectioners' sugar, if desired.

Makes 18 to 30 bars

Prominent Taste: *Sweet*	
If you want to reduce	eat
VATA	MORE
PITTA	SOME
KAPHA	LESS

OUTRAGEOUS OATMEAL COOKIES

◆

Oh, boy!

45 minutes to prepare

¾ cup turbinado sugar *(sweet)*
¾ cup (1½ sticks) unsalted butter, melted *(sweet)*
2 eggs *(sweet)*
1 tablespoon maple syrup *(sweet)*
2 cups organic unbleached white flour *(sweet, astringent)*
2 cups oats *(sweet)*

1 cup chopped dates *(sweet)*
1 cup raisins *(sweet)*
1 cup coconut *(sweet)*
1 tablespoon cinnamon *(pungent, bitter)*
1 teaspoon baking soda *(salty)*
¼ teaspoon sea salt *(salty)*

1. Preheat the oven to 325°F.
2. In a bowl, blend the first 4 ingredients. Add the remaining ingredients and mix well.
3. Drop by tablespoonfuls onto a sprayed baking sheet and bake 8 to 10 minutes. *Don't overcook. The cookies should be browned on the bottom only.*

Makes 36 cookies

Prominent Taste: *Sweet*	
If you want to reduce	*eat*
VATA	MORE
PITTA	MORE
KAPHA	LESS

𝒫RUNE 𝒞AKE

◆

Serve this warm with yogurt as part of a special breakfast.

1½ hours to prepare

2 cups chopped prunes *(sweet, sour)*

1¼ cups apple juice *(sweet, astringent)*

2 teaspoons cinnamon *(pungent, bitter)*

1 teaspoon nutmeg *(pungent, astringent)*

3 cups organic unbleached white flour *(sweet, astringent)*

2 teaspoons baking powder *(salty)*

½ cup molasses *(sweet)*

¼ cup plain nonfat yogurt *(sweet, sour)*

¼ cup ghee *(sweet)*

2 eggs *(sweet)*

1. Preheat the oven to 350° F. Butter or oil a 9 × 1-inch cake pan.
2. In a saucepan, poach the prunes in the apple juice until quite soft, then mash in a food processor. Cool.
3. Combine the cinnamon, nutmeg, flour, and baking powder in a mixing bowl.
4. In another bowl, blend the molasses, yogurt, ghee, and eggs. Add the mashed prunes, blending well. Add to the dry ingredients and mix.
5. Pour into the cake pan and bake for 1 hour, or until a knife inserted comes out clean. *Don't overcook.*

Makes 12 to 18 pieces

Prominent Taste: *Sweet*	
If you want to reduce	eat
VATA	SOME
PITTA	SOME
KAPHA	SOME

CONDIMENTS AND BEVERAGES

◆

This section covers important accessory foods to Ayurvedic cooking. Ghee, Paneer, lassi, chutneys, and *churans* are easy to make and serve a wide range of culinary uses.

CHURANS

GHEE

GINGER ELIXIR

LASSI

MORNING CHAI

PANEER CHEESE

CIRCUS SALSA

DATE-RAISIN CHUTNEY

MANGO CHUTNEY

TOMATO CHUTNEY

♥CHURANS

◆

*Making spice blends is a terrific way to personalize your foods.
Choose three or four spices and/or herbs that are appropriate for
each dosha. Then when seasoning vegetables, grains, and pastas
you can rest assured that those seasonings will balance your
dosha. The possible choices are:*

10 minutes to prepare

Vata

cardamom, cumin, ginger,
  cinnamon, salt, cloves, mustard
  seed, black pepper

Kapha

turmeric, ginger, mustard, cayenne,
  anise

Pitta

coriander, fennel, cumin, dill

$\mathcal{G}$HEE

◆

Ghee, clarified butter, is an essential ingredient in Ayurvedic cooking. It is easy to digest and contributes to the absorption of nutrients. It can be purchased in most health food and Indian stores. However, buying it is expensive. Once you make your own and discover how simple and delicious it is, you'll never buy it again.

45 minutes to prepare

1 or more pounds unsalted butter
(organic, if possible) *(sweet)*

1. Cut the butter into cubes and cook over medium-high heat in a heavy saucepan until melted. The butter will begin to foam and become white and frothy, making cracking and popping sounds. This is caused by the evaporation of moisture. Allow it to bubble in this way for about 10 minutes, or until the noises subside.
2. Now, watch this next part of the process carefully. Keep cooking. The butter will foam up a second time. At this point, the milk solids begin to separate and will turn golden brown. When the solids are browned, turn off the heat and let stand for about 15 minutes to allow to cool before pouring into jars. When pouring, strain the ghee through a cheesecloth. Discard the solids. (Note: Some Ayurvedic cooks use these solids for flavoring other foods.)
3. Store in airtight containers for up to 3 months in the refrigerator or 6 weeks at room temperature.

Prominent Taste: *Sweet*	
If you want to reduce	eat
VATA	MORE
PITTA	MORE
KAPHA	LESS

Ginger Elixir

◆

*Our kitchen staff prefers to give this digestive stimulant
the more romantic name of "The Aperitif."
It is consumed in small quantities before lunch or dinner.*

15 minutes to prepare

1 large piece fresh gingerroot
  (about 6 inches) *(pungent, sweet)*
Juice of 3 lemons *(sour, astringent)*

2 tablespoons honey *(sweet)*
Pinch of cayenne *(pungent)*

1. Cut the ginger into 1-inch pieces and press through a juicer. Blend with the remaining ingredients.
2. Store in an airtight container in the refrigerator for up to 3 days.

Makes about $1/2$ cup

Prominent Tastes: *Sweet, Pungent, Astringent*	
If you want to reduce	eat
VATA	SOME
PITTA	LESS
KAPHA	SOME

♥ Lassi

◆

Lassi is traditionally served at the end of a meal to aid digestion.
It is best consumed in warmer weather.

10 minutes to prepare

SWEET LASSI*

1 cup plain low-fat or nonfat
yogurt *(sweet, sour)*
¼ cup sweetener** *(sweet)*
2 to 3 cups cold filtered water

¼ teaspoon cardamom *(pungent,
sweet)*
2 teaspoons rose water, optional

1. Combine all the ingredients in a large jar and shake, or place in a blender and blend for 30 seconds.
2. Refrigerate until 30 minutes before serving.

Serves 4 to 6

Prominent Tastes: *Sweet, Sour*	
If you want to reduce	*eat*
VATA	MORE
PITTA	LESS
KAPHA	LESS

*Omit the sweetener for plain lassi.
For **Vata use barley or rice syrup, for **Pitta** use raw sugar, and for **Kapha** use honey.

❤ Morning Chai

◆

*For your morning kick start, try this soothing chai,
individually created for each dosha.*

20 minutes to prepare

2 tablespoons loose black tea or 2
black tea bags, optional *(bitter,
astringent)*

½ teaspoon cardamom *(pungent,
sweet)*

¼ teaspoon cinnamon *(pungent,
bitter)*

¼ teaspoon black peppercorns
(pungent)

¼ teaspoon ground ginger
(pungent, sweet)

¼ cup low-fat cow's milk, soy milk,
or Rice Dream* *(sweet)*

2 to 4 tablespoons sweetener*
(sweet)

1. In a large saucepan, bring 4 cups of water to a boil. Remove from the
   heat.
2. Add the loose tea or tea bags and the spices and steep in the pan or a
   teapot for 10 minutes. Add the milk and a sweetener for your dosha.

Makes 4 cups

Prominent Tastes: *Bitter, Pungent*	
If you want to reduce	*eat*
VATA	LESS
PITTA	SOME
KAPHA	MORE

*For **Vata** use cow's milk and barley or rice syrup, for **Pitta** use cow's milk and raw
sugar, and for **Kapha** use soy milk or Rice Dream and honey.

𝒫aneer 𝒞heese

◆

*Paneer is the Indian form of an old favorite, Italian ricotta. It is
easier to digest for all three doshas than most other cheeses.
Paneer is firmer than ricotta; it can be fried or used in fillings.*

25 minutes to prepare

1 gallon organic milk   1 quart cultured buttermilk

1. In a large pot, bring the milk to a boil over medium heat. Do not let it
   boil over. As it begins to foam, remove the pot from the heat and add
   the buttermilk. Stir gently. The curds and whey will begin to separate.
   Set aside while you line a colander with a large piece of cheesecloth.
2. Pour the cheese into the colander and strain until completely cooled.
   Gather the ends of the cloth and tightly squeeze it around the cheese,
   expelling as much liquid as possible. Allow the bag to rest in the colander for an additional hour or two to drain any further liquid.
3. For ricotta, put the cheese in an airtight container and refrigerate immediately. For Paneer, keep squeezing out the liquid until there just isn't
   any more. Remove the cheese from the cheesecloth and knead for 20
   seconds. Press flat in a shallow pan and refrigerate until needed.

Makes 2 cups

Prominent Tastes: *Sweet, Sour*	
If you want to reduce	*eat*
VATA	SOME
PITTA	SOME
KAPHA	LESS

CIRCUS SALSA

◆

This is a colorful name for a colorful dish. Serve it in summer when tomatoes, tomatillos, and corn are fresh.

25 minutes to prepare

1 pound roma tomatoes, chopped and drained well *(sweet, sour)*

½ pound tomatillos, chopped *(sweet, sour)*

1 small sweet red onion, finely chopped *(pungent, sweet)*

3 ears white corn, cut from the cob *(sweet)*

1 small garlic clove *(all but sour)*

1 fresh Anaheim chili or 1 can (2 ounces) diced green chilis *(pungent)*

1 firm avocado, chopped *(sweet)*

Juice of 1 lemon *(sour, astringent)*

Juice of 1 lime *(sour)*

¼ teaspoon sea salt *(salty)*

1 teaspoon turbinado sugar *(sweet)*

3 tablespoons chopped fresh cilantro *(pungent)*

1. In a large bowl, toss all the ingredients together. Refrigerate until 1 hour before serving.
2. Serve as a side dish with Black Bean Dip (page 41), pita bread or lavash, or your favorite spicy dish.

Serves 4 to 6

Prominent Tastes: *Sweet, Sour, Pungent*	
If you want to reduce	*eat*
VATA	MORE
PITTA	LESS
KAPHA	LESS

$\mathcal{D}$ATE-$\mathcal{R}$AISIN $\mathcal{C}$HUTNEY

◆

Try this with Curried Tempeh Salad (page 66).
The sweet chutney offsets the curry to perfection.

20 minutes to prepare

1 cup chopped dates *(sweet)*
¼ cup dried coconut *(sweet)*
½ cup raisins or currants *(sweet)*
1 teaspoon fennel seeds, bruised in
   a mortar and pestle *(pungent)*
Juice of 1 lemon *(sour, astringent)*

Juice of 1 lime *(sour)*
2-inch piece of fresh gingerroot,
   grated *(pungent, sweet)*
1 tablespoon finely chopped fresh
   cilantro *(pungent)*

1. Toss all the ingredients together in a bowl.
2. Cover and refrigerate for up to 3 days.

Serves 4 to 6

Prominent Tastes: *Sweet, Pungent, Sour*	
If you want to reduce	*eat*
VATA	SOME
PITTA	SOME
KAPHA	LESS

ℳᴀɴɢᴏ Cʜᴜᴛɴᴇʏ

◆

*Chutneys go with almost anything, from Cosmic Curry
Enchiladas (page 109) to Chili Chickpeas (page 44).
Make this fresh during mango season.*

20 minutes to prepare

2 underripe medium mangoes
 (sweet, sour)
1 tablespoon dried coconut *(sweet)*
2 tablespoons chopped fresh
 cilantro *(pungent)*

1 tablespoon grated fresh
 gingerroot *(pungent, sweet)*
⅛ teaspoon sea salt, optional *(salty)*
⅛ teaspoon hot pepper *(pungent)*

1. Peel the mangoes and carefully cut away from the seed. Cut into small,
   bite-size pieces. Toss in a bowl with the remaining ingredients.
2. Serve immediately or store, tightly covered, in the refrigerator for up to
   8 hours.

Serves 4 to 6

Prominent Tastes: *Sweet, Sour, Pungent*	
If you want to reduce	*eat*
VATA	MORE
PITTA	LESS
KAPHA	LESS

Tomato Chutney

◆

Try this with any curry dish.

40 minutes to prepare

1 tablespoon vegetable oil, preferably mustard *(pungent)*

2 tablespoon black mustard seeds *(pungent)*

1 garlic clove, minced *(all but sour)*

3 large, firm, ripe tomatoes, coarsely chopped *(sweet, sour)*

1 cup balsamic vinegar *(sour)*

1 cup dried onion flakes *(pungent, sweet)*

1 teaspoon cinnamon *(pungent, bitter)*

Pinch of sea salt (salty)

1 tablespoon dark molasses *(sweet)*

2 tablespoons grated fresh gingerroot *(pungent, sweet)*

6 whole cloves *(pungent)*

½ teaspoon chili flakes *(pungent)*

¼ cup finely chopped fresh cilantro *(pungent)*

1. In a large skillet, heat the oil for 1 minute. Add the mustard seeds and garlic. When the mustard seeds sputter and pop, add the tomatoes, vinegar, onion flakes, cinnamon, and salt. Bring to a boil.
2. Add the molasses, gingerroot, cloves, and chili flakes. Bring to a boil again, stirring frequently.
3. Cook for 10 minutes, or until the chutney thickens.
4. Cool to room temperature. Add the cilantro. Cover and refrigerate until 1 hour before serving.

Serves 4 to 6

Prominent Tastes: *Pungent, Sweet*	
If you want to reduce	*eat*
VATA	MORE
PITTA	LESS
KAPHA	SOME

ℬREAKFAST

◆

Western nutrition emphasizes the value of breakfast. Taking in fuel to start the day is important, but wait until your appetite calls before filling your stomach. One person may feel ravenous at 6:00 A.M.; another may not feel hunger until 10:00 A.M. Honor your digestive power.

GRANOLA

HOT BARLEY BREAKFAST
CEREAL

HOT BULGUR BREAKFAST
CEREAL

HOT OATS BREAKFAST
CEREAL

HOT RICE BREAKFAST
CEREAL

PLAIN MUESLI

♥ GRANOLA

◆

This is a low-fat version, with no added fat.

1 hour to prepare

2 cups organic rolled oats *(sweet)*

¼ cup sesame seeds *(sweet)*

¼ cup nuts, such as chopped almonds *(sweet, bitter)*, chopped walnuts *(sweet)*, or pine nuts *(sweet)*

¼ cup sunflower seeds *(sweet, bitter)*

2 tablespoons cinnamon *(pungent, bitter)*

1 teaspoon cardamom *(pungent, sweet)*

2 tablespoons grated orange peel *(bitter, sour)*

½ cup apple juice concentrate *(sweet, astringent)* or orange juice concentrate *(sweet, sour)*, heated

½ cup date pieces *(sweet)*

½ cup raisins or currants *(sweet)*

½ cup dried mixed fruit pieces *(sweet)*

½ cup coconut, optional *(sweet)*

1. Preheat the oven to 325° F.
2. In a mixing bowl, combine the oats, sesame seeds, nuts, spices, and orange peel. Mix well. Add the juice concentrate and mix well.
3. Spread the mixture on baking sheets and bake for about 45 minutes, stirring frequently, until toasted and dry.
4. Allow to cool before adding the fruits and optional coconut. Omit the coconut for even less fat. Store in an airtight container.

Makes about 8 cups

Prominent Taste: *Sweet*	
If you want to reduce	*eat*
VATA	MORE
PITTA	SOME
KAPHA	LESS

♥Hot Barley Breakfast Cereal

◆

This is best for **Kaphas** and **Pittas**.

1 hour to prepare

½ cup organic barley, rinsed *(sweet)*

Pinch of sea salt *(salty)*

1 teaspoon cinnamon *(pungent, bitter)*

¼ cup currants, optional *(sweet)*

Sweetener*, to taste *(sweet)*

Milk*, to taste *(sweet)*

1. In a saucepan, bring 3 cups of water to a boil. Add the barley and salt, cover, and simmer over very low heat for 1 hour, or until the barley is soft.
2. Add the cinnamon, optional currants, sweetener, and milk and let stand covered for 10 minutes. Add more milk, if desired.

Makes 3 cups

Prominent Taste: *Sweet*	
If you want to reduce	*eat*
VATA	SOME
PITTA	MORE
KAPHA	MORE

*For **Vata** use barley or rice syrup and cow's milk, for **Pitta** use raw sugar and cow's milk, and for **Kapha** use honey and soy milk.

♥Hot Bulgur Breakfast Cereal
◆

*This is best for **Vatas** and **Pittas**.*

30 minutes to prepare

½ cup bulgur wheat *(sweet)*

Pinch of sea salt *(salty)*

1 teaspoon cinnamon *(pungent, bitter)*

¼ cup currants, optional *(sweet)*

Sweetener*, to taste *(sweet)*

Milk*, to taste *(sweet)*

1. In a saucepan, bring 1½ cups of water to a boil. Add the bulgur and salt, cover, and simmer over very low heat for 25 minutes.
2. Add the cinnamon, optional currants, sweetener, and milk and let stand covered for 10 minutes. Add more milk, if desired.

Makes 2 cups

Prominent Taste: *Sweet*	
If you want to reduce	eat
VATA	MORE
PITTA	MORE
KAPHA	LESS

*For **Vata** use barley or rice syrup and cow's milk, for **Pitta** use raw sugar and cow's milk, and for **Kapha** use honey and soy milk.

❤Hot Oats Breakfast Cereal

❖

*This is good for **Vatas** and **Pittas**.*

30 minutes to prepare

½ cup organic steel cut oats *(sweet)*
Pinch of sea salt *(salty)*
1 teaspoon cinnamon *(pungent, bitter)*

¼ cup currants, optional *(sweet)*
Sweetener*, to taste *(sweet)*
Milk*, to taste *(sweet)*

1. In a saucepan, bring 3 cups of water to a boil. Add the oats and salt, cover, and simmer over very low heat for 25 minutes.
2. Add the cinnamon, optional currants, sweetener, and milk and let stand covered for 10 minutes. Add more milk, if desired.

Makes 3 cups

Prominent Taste: *Sweet*	
If you want to reduce	*eat*
VATA	MORE
PITTA	MORE
KAPHA	LESS

*For **Vata** use barley or rice syrup and cow's milk, for **Pitta** use raw sugar and cow's milk, and for **Kapha** use honey and soy milk or Rice Dream.

❤Hot Rice Breakfast Cereal

◆

This is good for all doshas.

30 minutes to prepare

½ cup organic basmati rice *(sweet)*
Pinch of sea salt *(salty)*
1 teaspoon cinnamon *(pungent, bitter)*

¼ cup currants, optional *(sweet)*
Sweetener*, to taste *(sweet)*
Milk*, to taste *(sweet)*

1. In a saucepan, bring 1 cup of water to a boil. Add the rice and salt, cover, and simmer over very low heat for 20 minutes.
2. Add the cinnamon, optional currants, sweetener, and milk and let stand covered for 10 minutes. Add more milk, if desired.

Makes 1 ½ cups

Prominent Taste: *Sweet*	
If you want to reduce	eat
VATA	SOME
PITTA	SOME
KAPHA	SOME

*For **Vata** use barley or rice syrup and cow's milk, for **Pitta** use raw sugar and cow's milk, and for **Kapha** use honey and soy milk or Rice Dream.

❦Plain Muesli

◆

If served with nonfat milk or yogurt, this is a great fat-free breakfast.

45 minutes to prepare

2 cups organic rolled oats *(sweet)*

1. Preheat the oven to 325° F.
2. Spread the oats on a baking sheet and bake for about 45 minutes, stirring frequently, until toasted and dry. Allow to cool. The muesli may be stored in an airtight container for several weeks.

Makes 2 cups

Prominent Tastes: *Sweet, Sour, Pungent*	
If you want to reduce	*eat*
VATA	MORE
PITTA	SOME
KAPHA	LESS

Chapter

5

PURIFICATION AND REJUVENATION

EATING TO DETOXIFY/EATING TO REJUVENATE

The idea that we store impurities in our mind-body system as a result of a stressed metabolism is new to science. Western medicine has only recently begun addressing issues like free radicals as an important feature of aging and illness. We are now learning that while our cells are functioning, we create very reactive chemicals that alter proteins and carbohydrates in our tissues, rendering them indigestible. Over time, this stuff gunks up our cells, leading to disease and death.

Ayurveda seems to have anticipated this discovery thousands of years ago when it described a toxic substance called *ama* as the product of incomplete digestion. Over time, *ama* accumulates, blocking the channels of circulation. When the channels are obstructed, the life force *(prana)* cannot reach the cells and tissues, leading to degeneration.

There are many classic signs and symptoms of accumulated *ama*. These include:

fatigue

weak digestion

bad breath

a coated tongue

general pain

weakness

difficulty concentrating

depression

irritability

If we are experiencing any of these symptoms, it's a sign that we've been accumulating toxicity, which is making our minds dull and our bodies weak. If we see a medical doctor at this time, complaining of fatigue or discomfort, any laboratory test that is ordered is likely to be normal. According to Ayurveda, this is the best time to put some attention on cleansing the system because it is much harder to reestablish health once a definite imbalance has gotten a foothold. Clearing the mind and body from *ama* at this stage is true disease prevention and health promotion.

WHEN TO CONSIDER A DETOXIFICATION PROGRAM

Anytime we are challenged physically or emotionally, we have the tendency to accumulate toxicity. If we have been through a major recent life event such as a change in residence, job, or relationship, the chances are that we have used up some life energy and could use a simplified nutritional plan for a while. Any intense major happening like a graduation or wedding is usually accompanied by some temporary disruption in our eating habits and sleeping pattern. These are times that our digestive power is weakened and *ama* can accumulate. Long-distance traveling is another experience that can be energy consuming, and it is helpful to follow a detoxification program for a day or two after a long trip.

If we have faced a recent health problem such as surgery or infection, we almost certainly have accumulated emotional and physical stress and can use some detoxification. This is particularly true if we have needed to be on one or more medicines for a time.

If we have been overeating recently and seem to be packing on a few more pounds than we'd prefer, it probably reflects some lack of mind-body integration due to subtle toxin accumulation. Shifting to a detox program for a few days will reestablish our mind-body connection. Whenever we find that our energy level is not what we think it should be and our bio-rhythms are out of sync, it's a good idea to slow things down for a couple of days and focus on purifying with an *ama*-reducing program.

THE AMA-REDUCING PLAN

The basic plan is to simplify. By only taking in foods that are easy to metabolize, we allow our digestive forces to focus on burning up accumulated toxins. In Ayurveda, the principle of digestive power is known as *agni.* This Sanskrit word also means "fire," which is an interesting way to think about our ability to digest what we take in. If our internal "fires" are strong, we can burn what we take in, creating abundant energy and healthy tissues. If our "fires" are weak, our digestion becomes delicate and we aren't able to create the energy we need. We also generate *ama,* which can be thought of as the smoke and charred remains of a weak fire. The goal of the detoxification program is to "reset" our digestive fires and burn up accumulated impurities.

The food we eat and the manner and environment in which we eat it all influence our digestive power. During the *ama*-reducing program, we pay attention to all these aspects of eating and digesting. These are the recommendations:

- All food should be freshly prepared, nutritious, and appetizing; avoid canned foods and leftovers.

- Foods should be lighter in quality, such as rice, soups, and lentils.

- Favor freshly steamed or *very* lightly sautéed vegetables.

- Avoid fried foods.

- Avoid cold foods and drinks.

- Minimize dairy products.

- Avoid fermented foods and drinks. These include vinegar, pickled condiments, cheeses, and alcohol.

- Keep oils to a minimum.

- Favor lighter grains, such as barley or millet.

- Avoid refined sugars; small amounts of honey may be used but should not be cooked with or heated.

- Avoid most nuts, which are oily, heavy, and usually salted; sunflower, pumpkin, or sesame seeds may be taken in small amounts.

- If you cannot avoid animal products, favor the white meat of turkey or chicken; avoid red meats, particularly pork and beef.

- Drink plenty of fluids during the detox program. We recommend preparing a ginger tea by grating 1 teaspoon of fresh gingerroot into 1 pint of boiling water. If you prepare this in a Thermos bottle in the morning, you can sip it throughout the day. Ginger, known in Ayurveda as the "universal medicine," is cleansing and purifying. If you can't find fresh ginger, sip warm water throughout the day.

- Aloe vera juice is another readily available natural detoxifier. Taken in a dose of two tablespoons twice per day for five to seven days, it is restorative to the immune system, particularly after a course of antibiotics.

AMA-REDUCING HERBS AND SPICES

Certain herbs and spices are very effective in helping the body detoxify. Herbs with a predominantly bitter taste help to reduce *ama* while those with a pungent taste help to "burn it up." Readily available bitter herbs include turmeric, coriander, rosemary, dill, and fenugreek. Herbs and spices with a pungent taste can be classified as being warm or hot. The warm spices, such as cumin, cardamom, coriander, basil, and fennel, will not aggravate people with a tendency toward high **Pitta**. The hot spices like cayenne, black pepper, dried ginger, and mustard can quickly incinerate *ama* but should be used cautiously if **Pitta** is predominant.

DURATION OF THE CLEANSING PROGRAM

The *ama*-reducing plan is recommended three times per year, at the beginning of autumn, winter, and spring. People with predominantly **Vata** constitutions should follow the diet for one week at a time. People with **Pitta** constitutions may follow it for two to four weeks. If you are predominately **Kapha**, you can benefit from the *ama*-reducing program intermittently throughout the year, as it most closely resembles a standard **Kapha**-balancing regimen.

Although many of the general principles of the *ama*-reducing diet are beneficial at all times, it wouldn't be any fun to be always so restrictive. When you feel your energy level is rising and your digestion improving, begin to add some dairy, oils, nuts, and heavier grains. Occasional helpings of fried or fermented foods can add variety to a meal.

LIQUID DIET

An easy way to follow a cleansing diet is to take everything in the form of a liquid or puree for a day. This means drinking the fresh juices of fruits and vegetables throughout the day and taking thin soups that have been blended. Whenever possible, use freshly squeezed rather than bottled or frozen juices, as *prana* is always highest in fresh foods.

Apples and citrus fruits are available year round in most areas and easily make fresh juices. Pitted fruits (peaches, plums, nectarines) also make wonderful juices, but will not be available in all seasons. With a good juicer or extractor, delicious juices can be made from carrots, beets, and celery. Mixing fruit and vegetable juices together can create very appetizing combinations, such as apple-carrot or apple-beet.

Making up a thin vegetable soup and then blending it can provide a nourishing meal that is also very easy to digest. Adding some mung beans to the blend insures that all the tastes and nutritional components are included.

We recommend using a liquid diet for one day at a time. If your mind body type is predominantly **Vata,** and you feel fine going for a day without solid foods, then following the program one day per month is recommended. If you are a **Pitta,** two or three times per month is of value. If you are a **Kapha** type, then as often as one day per week can be helpful in reducing the tendency to accumulate toxins.

VEGETABLE BROTH

◆

40 minutes to prepare

1 carrot, cut into pieces *(sweet, pungent)*
2 celery stalks, cut into pieces *(bitter, astringent)*
2 cups chopped spinach *(bitter)*
1 potato, quartered *(astringent)*

Dash of asafoetida (hing) *(pungent)*
⅛ teaspoon tarragon *(pungent)*
2 cups purified water
1 tablespoon Bragg's Liquid Aminos *(astringent, salty)*

1. In a soup pot, combine all the ingredients and bring to a boil. Simmer for 20 minutes.
2. Strain the vegetables for a clear broth or blend in a food processor or with a hand-held soup blender for a thick soup.

Makes 3 cups

Prominent Tastes: *Pungent, Bitter, Astringent*	
If you want to reduce	*eat*
VATA	SOME
PITTA	SOME
KAPHA	MORE

$\mathcal{B}$EET $\mathcal{B}$ROTH

◆

1 hour to prepare

4 cups purified water

1 tablespoon vegetable broth powder *(all)*

2 pounds beets, washed and chopped *(bitter, sweet)*

⅛ teaspoon grated fresh gingerroot *(pungent, sweet)*

⅛ teaspoon grated orange zest *(bitter)*

Pinch of asafoetida (hing) *(pungent)*

1. In a soup pot, combine all the ingredients and bring to a boil. Simmer for 30 to 40 minutes, until the beets are soft.
2. Strain for a clear beet broth or blend in a food processor or with a hand-held soup blender for a thick soup.

Makes 4 cups

Prominent Tastes: *Sweet, Bitter, Pungent*	
If you want to reduce	*eat*
VATA	SOME
PITTA	SOME
KAPHA	MORE

GREEN SOUP

◆

20 minutes to prepare

3 pounds spinach, washed and chopped *(bitter)*

2 celery stalks, cut into pieces *(bitter, astringent)*

¼ cup chopped parsley *(pungent, astringent)*

¼ cup chopped cilantro *(pungent, astringent)*

4 cups purified water

1 tablespoon Bragg's Liquid Aminos *(astringent, salty)*

⅛ teaspoon tarragon *(pungent)*

1. In a soup pot, combine all the ingredients and bring to a boil.
2. Strain for a clear broth or blend in a food processor or with a hand-held soup blender for a thick soup.

Makes 4 cups

Prominent Tastes: *Bitter, Pungent, Astringent*	
If you want to reduce	*eat*
VATA	SOME
PITTA	MORE
KAPHA	MORE

ᐯEGETABLE ᒍUICE

◆

15 minutes to prepare

1 carrot *(sweet, pungent)*
1 beet *(bitter, sweet)*
1 bunch spinach *(bitter)*

Pinch of sea salt
Purified water, as necessary for
thinning

1. Press the vegetables through a juicer. Discard the pulp. Add salt. Thin with water, if desired.
2. Drink immediately.

Makes 1 to 2 cups

Prominent Tastes: *Bitter, Sweet*	
If you want to reduce	*eat*
VATA	SOME
PITTA	SOME
KAPHA	SOME

REJUVENATION

According to Ayurveda there are certain foods that are rich in *prana* and therefore recommended on a daily basis. These *prana*-rich foods are **milk, almonds, honey,** and **ghee** (clarified butter). Adding just a small amount of these nourishing substances to your diet will improve your vitality. A great energy booster that can be taken in the morning or later in the day is an Almond-Banana Shake. If you are recovery from a debilitating illness, trying to gain weight, or just want an energy boost, this drink is delicious and satisfying.

ALMOND-BANANA SHAKE

◆

1 cup low-fat or whole milk *(sweet)*

1 whole banana *(sweet)*

2 tablespoons almond butter *(sweet, bitter)*

1 teaspoon honey *(sweet)*

½ teaspoon ghee *(sweet)*

Blend all of the ingredients together.

Serves 1

Prominent Taste: *Sweet*	
If you want to reduce	*eat*
VATA	MORE
PITTA	SOME
KAPHA	LESS

There is an entire Ayurvedic science of revitalizers, or *Rasayanas,* which has explored the rejuvenative value of foods for thousands of years. Some of the fruit and herb formulas described thousands of years ago are available today. The most famous one is known as *Chavan Prash,* which has a fruit known as *amalaki (Emblic myrobalan)* as its major constituent. This fruit has *ten times* the vitamin C per gram of pulp than an orange and, when combined with more than forty other herbs and spices, is a powerful restorative. It has potent antioxidant properties, which may explain its long-held reputation as an antiaging formula. It is usually available as an herbal jam that can be taken plain, spread on bread, or mixed with warm milk or water.

If you put your attention on reducing the toxins in your life and accepting only nourishing influences, you will notice a big improvement in your physical and mental clarity. Taking the time to focus on detoxification and rejuvenation pays off. You'll accomplish things more easily because you will have more energy and will enjoy whatever you're doing more.

High Energy Snack

◆

10 minutes to prepare

½ cup crushed toasted almonds *(sweet, bitter)*

½ cup toasted coconut *(sweet)*

2 tablespoons toasted sesame seeds, plus additional, for rolling *(sweet)*

3 tablespoons honey* *(sweet)*

½ cup dried fruit (currants, dates, cherries, blueberries) *(sweet, sour, astringent)*

1. In a food processor, combine the almonds, coconut, 2 tablespoons sesame seeds, honey, and dried fruit and process for about 30 seconds, until well blended and pulverized.
2. By the teaspoonful, form into balls and roll in additional sesame seeds. These can be stored in the refrigerator in an airtight container for several days.

Makes 10 to 12 medium-sized balls

Prominent Tastes: *Sweet, Astringent*	
If you want to reduce	*eat*
VATA	MORE
PITTA	SOME
KAPHA	SOME

*For **Pitta** and **Kapha** use honey and for **Vata** use maple syrup.

Tofu-Nut Burger

◆

30 minutes to prepare

1 pound firm tofu, drained well
  (sweet, astringent)
¼ cup toasted pine nuts *(sweet)*
¼ cup toasted almonds *(sweet,
  bitter)*
¼ cup toasted sunflower seeds
  (sweet, bitter)
1 egg *(sweet)*

2 tablespoons Bragg's Liquid
  Aminos *(astringent, salty)*
¼ cup dry wheat bread crumbs,
  plus additional bread crumbs
  (sweet)
¼ cup chopped celery *(bitter,
  astringent)*
1 tablespoon ghee, optional *(sweet)*

1. Preheat the oven to 400° F.
2. In a large bowl, crumble the tofu.
3. Place the pine nuts, almonds, and sunflower seeds in a food processor and process until pulverized. Combine with the tofu, egg, Bragg's Liquid Aminos, ¼ cup bread crumbs, and celery. Form into patties.
4. Place additional bread crumbs in a small bowl. Place each patty in the bowl with the bread crumbs, patting gently on each side, to pick up the crumbs. Fry in ghee, if desired, or bake in the oven for 10 minutes.

Serves 2 to 4

Prominent Tastes: *Sweet, Bitter, Astringent*	
If you want to reduce	*eat*
VATA	MORE
PITTA	SOME
KAPHA	LESS

Sweet Lassi

◆

5 minutes to prepare

1 cup plain nonfat yogurt *(sweet, sour)*

½ cup rose water or purified water

¼ teaspoon cardamom *(pungent, sweet)*

¼ teaspoon cinnamon *(pungent, bitter)*

1 tablespoon honey or maple syrup *(sweet)*

Combine all the ingredients and shake or stir well. Make fresh daily.

Serves 2 to 4

Prominent Tastes: *Sweet, Pungent*	
If you want to reduce	*eat*
VATA	SOME
PITTA	LESS
KAPHA	LESS

SPINACH AND PANEER CASSEROLE

❖

45 minutes to prepare

1 teaspoon ghee *(sweet)*

2 large leeks, washed and chopped *(pungent, sweet)*

3 pounds fresh washed spinach *(bitter)*

1 teaspoon each cumin, coriander, turmeric *(pungent)*

1 tablespoon Bragg's Liquid Aminos *(astringent, salty)*

1 cup Paneer cheese, cut into small pieces *(sweet, sour)*

1 egg *(sweet)*

½ cup crushed toasted almonds *(sweet, bitter)*

¼ cup bread crumbs *(sweet)*

1. Preheat the oven to 350° F.
2. In a large skillet, heat the ghee to the smoking point. Sauté the leeks until soft and browned. Add the spinach and cook until slightly wilted. Remove from the heat.
3. Add the remaining ingredients except 2 tablespoons of bread crumbs.
4. Pour into a lightly oiled or sprayed casserole dish and sprinkle with the remaining bread crumbs. Bake for 25 minutes, or until the crumbs are browned and the casserole is bubbling.

Serves 2 to 4

Prominent Tastes: *Sweet, Bitter, Pungent*	
If you want to reduce	*eat*
VATA	SOME
PITTA	SOME
KAPHA	SOME

Chapter

6

COOKING SINGLE

Living alone has its nourishment hazards: why is it that the most important body we know, our own, gets the least attention? We eat on the run, eat junk food, eat less than we should, eat *leftovers* or eat out. Cooking single can be a rewarding, self-nourishing ritual. Sit down to a well-balanced meal by yourself at a beautifully set table. Look at the food and give thanks for the gifts of life and sustenance. While you are eating, concentrate on the act of eating itself. Chew slowly, swallowing each bite before you lift another forkful into your mouth. Feel the food enter your cells as life force. Don't watch television. Don't read. Don't answer the phone. Become the ritual of eating. It's difficult, isn't it? We are used to distraction, diversion, and entertainment. We hurry through the meal, thinking there must be something more important to do than sit alone in a room with a plate of spaghetti. We bolt down the meal, throw the plate in the dishwasher, and run out the door.

In this chapter, we offer a few menus and recipes for one. Take care of yourself.

M E N U

PASTA PRIMAVERA *(sweet, astringent)*
SALAD OF BABY GREENS WITH YOUR DOSHIC DRESSING
(bitter, astringent, sour)
WHOLE WHEAT CHAPPATIS *(sweet)*

PASTA PRIMAVERA

◆

25 minutes to prepare

1 carrot *(sweet, pungent)*
1 broccoli stalk *(bitter, astringent)*
1 celery stalk *(bitter, astringent)*
5 green beans *(sweet, astringent)*
1 tablespoon oil, olive for **Vata** and
   Pitta, sunflower for **Kapha** *(sweet)*
½ bunch fresh basil *(pungent)*

¼ teaspoon asafoetida (hing)
   (pungent)
Juice of 1 lemon *(sour, astringent)*
4 sun-dried tomatoes, chopped
   (sweet, sour)
1 cup cooked pasta of your choice
   (sweet)
Grated Parmesan cheese *(sweet)*

1. Cut the carrot, broccoli, celery, and green beans into bite-size pieces. In a hot skillet, sauté quickly in the oil. Toss in the basil, asafoetida, lemon juice, and tomatoes.
2. Serve over warm pasta, adding Parmesan cheese.

Serves 1

Prominent Tastes: *Sweet, Astringent*	
If you want to reduce	*eat*
VATA	MORE
PITTA	SOME
KAPHA	LESS

M E N U

A DIFFERENT PESTO *(all)*
PASTA *(sweet)*
STEAMED VEGETABLE *(bitter, astringent)*
BAKED APPLE *(sweet)*

A DIFFERENT PESTO

◆

20 minutes to prepare

¼ cup fresh spinach, washed and stemmed *(bitter)*

½ avocado, cut into pieces *(sweet)*

¼ cup fresh cilantro *(pungent)*

¼ cup fresh basil *(pungent)*

¼ cup fresh parsley *(pungent, astringent)*

2 tablespoons lemon juice *(sour, astringent)*

2 tablespoons pine nuts *(sweet)*

Salt *(salty)*

Pepper *(pungent)*

1 cup cooked pasta of your choice *(sweet)*

Combine all the ingredients except the pasta in a food processor and blend well. Serve with warm pasta.

Serves 1

Prominent Tastes: *All*	
If you want to reduce	*eat*
VATA	MORE
PITTA	SOME
KAPHA	SOME

ℬAKED 𝒜PPLE

◆

45 minutes to prepare

1 Pippin or Granny Smith apple
(sweet, astringent)

½ teaspoon ghee *(sweet)*

2 teaspoons ground pine nuts
(sweet)

1 teaspoon maple syrup *(sweet)*

¼ teaspoon cinnamon *(pungent)*

¼ cup unfiltered apple juice *(sweet)*

1. Preheat the oven to 400°F.
2. Peel the top of the apple about ⅓ of the way down and cut out a 1-inch piece from the center core. Mix the ghee, nuts, maple syrup, and cinnamon together and put in the well in the center of apple.
3. Place in a small baking dish with the apple juice, cover with foil, and bake about 30 minutes. Uncover, baste with apple juice, and bake until soft, about 15 more minutes.

Serves 1

Prominent Taste: *Sweet*	
If you want to reduce	*eat*
VATA	SOME
PITTA	SOME
KAPHA	SOME

Chapter

7

MENU PLANNING

The following suggested menus are derived from the recipes in this book. We offer these to help you create balance throughout your week in planning Ayurvedic meals.

BREAKFAST

We acknowledge that breakfast is different for everyone. However, we suggest that the following items often be included for balance:

Granola or hot cereal with a pinch of salt (sweet, salty)

Morning Chai (bitter, astringent, pungent)

Yogurt (sweet, sour)

Fruit (sweet, astringent)

LUNCH OR DINNER

According to Ayurveda, lunch should be the main meal of the day. We understand busy lifestyles often prevent our eating at home or even eating where or when we wish. The options below give you examples of the variety and balance to look for in your meals out or in home meal planning. Time usually allows for more attention to dinner preparation. A calm, gentle atmosphere adds to the experience. Remember, *don't stress!* Mealtime is a celebration, not a drama. Choose items carefully, relax, and enjoy.

A Different Pesto (with pasta)

Spinach Greens with Gorgonzola

French Bread

Lemon Bars

◆

Mushroom Stroganoff (with basmati rice)

Classic Chopped Salad

Anadama Bread

Glazed Pear Tart

◆

Cosmic Curry (with basmati rice)

Cucumber Raita

Whole Wheat Chappatis

Blueberry Bliss Balls

◆

Veggie Burgers

Salad Greens with Doshic Dressing of Choice

Baked Apples

◆

Cheeseless Lasagne

Leeks and Limas

Italianate Muffins

Chocolate Chip Cookies

◆

Acorn Squash Soup

Chappati Crisp Salad

Ginger-Molasses Cookies

◆

Vegetable Chow Mein

Orange Almond Rice

Fresh Blueberry Cake

◆

Tofu Satay (with basmati rice)

Orange Almond Spinach

Naan

Shakti Date Balls

◆

Red Lentil Dahl

Curried Tempeh Salad

Pita Bread

Pear-Date Raita

Baklava

◆

Watermelon Soup
(with Beets and Orange)

Vegetarian Niçoise

Goody Muffins

Date Bars

Chapter

8

ORCHESTRATING
A FEAST

We describe tantra as a "composition in consciousness with four-part harmony: *Kriya*, ritual; *Carya*, demeanor; *Yoga*, integration of mind, body, and spirit; and *Anuttara*, understanding." These practices, when carried with you into the kitchen, create an atmosphere of wholeness and unity. When we begin to understand the completeness of our being through these practices, we begin to share in the unity and spirit of all things.

Although we express the idea that all meals are an opportunity for celebrating nourishment and that every act of eating can be a special occasion, we acknowledge that there are moments when more time is available and more thought given to the experience.

Orchestrating a meal gives you the opportunity to compose a tantric melody. It can be sung by a choir. It can be whispered, like the chanting of monks. It is a gift of creation and a process of celebration.

One of the most important aspects of the creation of a meal is organization. If you are baking bread, making a sumptuous dessert, cooking rice, and creating appetizers, you are probably looking forward to an evening soiree, Sunday brunch, or a gathering of friends. This not only means cooking a meal but arranging flowers, ironing napkins, and blow-drying your hair. Don't despair. It can come together easily if certain organizational steps are taken, if your heart is in the right place, and if you relax.

Preparing Ayurvedically balanced menus includes the six tastes, *churans,* accompanying music, flowers, and a beautiful table. The spirit with which you begin is the spirit that carries through the entire experience. Are you nervous? Not to worry. Begin with the ritual (thought) that this is a divine moment in creation. Make your shopping list while sipping tea and listening to melodic music. Plan a menu with six tastes represented, list the ingredients, then look out the window at a flower. Remind yourself that this is a party, not a summit meeting, and you are honored to be the party giver.

While you are shopping, buy fresh flowers (or collect them from nature if you can)— some for the table and some for you in the kitchen. Take your own bags to save a tree. If you are able to shop at farmers' markets, smile and talk with the farmers; let them know how much you appreciate the beautiful tomatoes grown with their love.

Upon arriving home, take all your ingredients out of the bags and pile them up on the counters, arranging a tableau of peppers, potatoes, tomatoes, nectarines, and flowers, or whatever you have chosen. To look at the bounty of produce on your counters is to partake in the abundance that is life. Place a fresh flower in a vase, light a candle, and prepare yourself to become the task of washing vegetables, kneading dough, and beating eggs. Listen to music. Be in love. With whom? With yourself and life, of course.

So, here you are, set to go. The menu is planned. The marketing is done. The candle is lit. The ritual is begun. Now what? If you are not already comfortable in the kitchen, this moment can be disconcerting. How is this done so that everything comes out at the same time? How can I do all this and still have time to rest, shower, and arrange the table?

Look at your menu. It looks something like this:

Acorn Squash Soup

Mushroom Stroganoff over basmati rice

Classic Chopped Salad

French Bread

Glazed Pear Tart

Begin to take it apart by its components. The bread takes the longest, but it does not need to go into the oven for at least 1½ hours, after it has risen. The squash needs to be baked. The pears need poaching. The salad needs washing and chopping. Make the dressing. Defrost the pastry.

Make an outline of what has to be done. For example:

Preheat the oven.

Cut the squash and bake it.

Make the bread dough and set it aside to rise (near a warm stove).

Peel the pears and poach in the juices.

Wash the mushrooms and other stroganoff ingredients.

Wash the vegetables for chopped salad.

When the bread dough is doubled, punch it down, make loaves, and set aside to rise.

Remove the pears from the pot to cool and reduce the juice to syrup.

Remove the cooked squash from the oven and cool.

Chop the stroganoff ingredients and set aside.

Chop the salad ingredients and place in a bowl.

Place the risen loaves in the oven.

Make the dressing.

Finish the soup.

Turn off the heat under the reduced syrup and cool.

Take a break, have lunch, sip tea.

Arrange the flowers.

Remove the bread from the oven to cool.

Defrost the pastry dough.

Finish the tart.

Take another break. The main body of work is finished. Take a bath, meditate, relax. Make sure you give yourself time for this. Your nurturing of yourself is every bit as important as the nourishment you are preparing for your friends or family.

Refreshed, you reenter your studio of nourishment and begin the final preparation. Set the table, light the candles, fluff up the sofa pillows.

When your guests arrive, you are happy and relaxed and your kitchen is sparkling clean, awaiting last-minute dinner preparations; all you have left to do is

Finish the stroganoff.

Cook the rice.

Toss the salad.

Be charming.

Invite friends into the kitchen to talk while you finish your preparations. Let them share in your enjoyment of the abundance in which they are about to take part: the crusty loaves cooling on racks on the counter; the prepared salad in a beautiful bowl, the dressing in a little jar beside it; the vegetables, ready to be sautéed, nested on a colorful platter. Your temple of creation includes the energy of your guests at this point, and they can't help but be honored by your effort.

We request one final thing: Enjoy yourself.

CELEBRATE

◆

Food is a celebration of life. Whether you are packing your lunch in the morning, planning a dinner party for eight, or creating a wedding feast for 100, give attention to the details in every step. Honor the ritual of preparation; honor the ceremony of eating; honor yourself and the process of transformation that you are while you eat. You are a beautiful creation, combined of body, mind, and spirit. When you are in your studio of nourishment, you have the opportunity to contribute richness and harmony to the act of eating. As a cook, you hold in your hands the tools of sustenance. As an artist of nourishment, you are creating sacred space and sacred food. Be on holy ground. Be at peace. Be love itself. Be well.

A P P E N D I X

Glossary of Terms

A G N I :   digestive power

A M A :   toxic residues of incompletely metabolized substances

A Y U R V E D A :   science or knowledge of life

B R A H M A N :   spirit; pure potentiality

C H U R A N S :   spices blended for each individual dosha

D H A R M A :   purpose in life

D O S H A :   mind-body principle

> *V A T A :*   the dosha responsible for all movement in the body

> *P I T T A :*   the dosha responsible for metabolism or transformation in the body

> *K A P H A :*   the dosha responsible for structure and lubrication of the body

P R A N A :   life force

R A J A S :   principles of energy and acitvity

R A S A :   the essence of body tissue; taste; emotions

S A T T V A :   principle of creativity and clarity

T A M A S I C :   principle of intertia, resistance

T A N T R A :   the web of life; practices to become aware of the spiritual nature of all things

> *A N U T T A R A :*   understanding

> *C A R Y A :*   demeanor

> *K R I Y A :*   ritual

> *Y O G A :*   integration of mind, body, and spirit

V E D A :   knowledge of creation in its unmanifest and manifest expressions

Suggested Reading

The books listed below are valuable resources for anyone interested in the further study of Auyrveda. We heartfully thank our teachers for providing this information. We recommend these books for your home library:

Ageless Body Timeless Mind
Deepak Chopra, M.D.

Ayurveda: The Science of Self-Healing
Vasant Lad

The Ayurvedic Cookbook
Amadea Morningstar with Urmila Desai

The Book of Ayurveda: A Holistic Approach to Health and Longevity
Judith H. Morrison

The Healing Cuisine: India's Art of Ayurvedic Cooking
Harish Johari

Perfect Weight: The Complete Mind-Body Program for Achieving and Maintaining Your Ideal Weight
Deepak Chopra, M.D.

Tantra for the West
Marc Allen

The Yoga of Herbs: An Ayurvedic Guide to Herbal Medicine
David Frawley and Vasant Lad

Balance of Tastes Chart

O f the six tastes, sweet, sour, and salty are the most predominant in our usual diet. Pungent, bitter, and astringent are taken in less quantity but are very important for their balancing influence on our physiology. Pungent taste is commonly obtained through the hot spices such as pepper, chilis, ginger, and mustard but is also present in many herbs like basil, sage, and cinnamon. The bitter taste is very common in nature and most medicinal herbs are predominantly bitter, but we are naturally less attracted to bitter taste and tend to use it in smaller quantities as a culinary spice. Although most of us don't love a bitter taste, it has a very important influence on digestion by serving to cleanse our system of toxins. Leafy greens are the most important food source of bitter taste, but it is also prominent in commonly used herbs and spices such as dill, fenugreek, turmeric, and coriander. Astringent taste is relatively rare. Lentils, beans, and dahls are the most available sources of astringent taste. The puckery feeling in your mouth after a great cup of black tea demonstrates the astringent influence. Fruits such as pomegranate, apples, and cranberries are astringent. Herbs and spices that carry the astringent taste include sage, cinnamon, and nutmeg.

The following Balance of Tastes Chart characterizes commonly available foods, herbs, and spices according to their Ayurvedic energetics. For a more detailed description of their specific effects, we refer you to the recommended reading list on page 208.

VEGETABLES	TASTE	VATA	PITTA	KAPHA
Artichokes	sweet, astringent	Less	More	Some
Asparagus	sweet, bitter, astringent	Some	More	More
Bean Sprouts	astringent, sweet	Less	More	More
Beans (green)	sweet, astringent	Less	More	More
Beets	bitter, sweet	More	Some	More
Bell Peppers	sweet, astringent	Less	Some	Some
Broccoli	bitter, astringent	Less	More	More
Brussels Sprouts	astringent, sweet	Less	More	More
Cabbage	astringent, sweet	Less	More	More
Carrots	sweet, pungent	More	Some	More
Cauliflower	sweet, astringent	Some	More	Some
Celery	bitter, astringent	Some	More	More
Chilis (hot pepper)	pungent	More	Less	More
Cilantro	pungent	More	More	More
Corn	sweet	Less	Some	Some
Cucumbers	sweet, astringent	Some	More	Less
Eggplants	bitter	Some	Some	Some
Fennel	pungent	More	Less	More
Jerusalem Artichokes	sweet	More	More	Less
Jicama	sweet	More	More	Less
Lettuce	bitter, astringent	Less	More	More
Mushrooms	sweet, astringent	Less	More	More
Mustard Greens	pungent, bitter	More	Less	More
Okra	sweet	More	More	Some
Onions, cooked (leeks, scallions, chives, shallots)	sweet, pungent	Some	Some	More
Onions, raw (leeks, scallions, chives, shallots)	sweet, pungent	Less	Less	Less
Parsley	pungent, astringent	More	Some	Some
Peas (Green or Snow)	sweet, astringent	Less	More	More
Potatoes	astringent	Less	Some	Some
Radishes	bitter	More	Some	More
Seaweed	salty, astringent	More	Some	Some
Spinach (Chard)	bitter	Some	Some	Some

VEGETABLES	TASTE	VATA	PITTA	KAPHA
Squash				
Acorn	sweet	Less	Some	Some
Winter	sweet	Less	Some	Less
Zucchini, Yellow				
Crookneck	sweet	Less	More	Less
Sweet Potatoes	sweet	More	Some	Less
Tomatoes	sweet, sour	Less	Some	Some
Turnips/Rutabagas	astringent	Less	Some	More

GRAINS	TASTE	VATA	PITTA	KAPHA
Barley	sweet	Some	More	More
Buckwheat	sweet	Some	Some	Some
Corn	sweet	Some	Some	Some
Couscous	sweet, astringent	Less	More	Less
Granola				
Dried grains	sweet, astringent	Less	Some	More
Millet	sweet	Some	Some	Some
Oats	sweet	More	More	Less
Quinoa	sweet, astringent	Some	Some	More
Rice				
Basmati	sweet	More	More	Some
Brown	sweet	More	Some	Less
Refined, White	sweet	Some	Some	Less
Rye	sweet, astringent	Less	Some	Some
Spelt	sweet, astringent	More	More	Some
White Flour	sweet, astringent	Less	Less	Less
Whole Wheat Flour	sweet, astringent	More	More	Less

HERBS, SPICES	TASTE	VATA	PITTA	KAPHA
Allspice	pungent	More	Less	More
Anise	pungent	Less	Less	More
Asafoetida (hing)	pungent	More	Less	More
Basil	pungent	More	Some	More
Bay Leaves	pungent	More	Less	More
Black Pepper	pungent	Some	Less	More
Calamus	pungent	More	Less	More
Caraway	pungent	More	Some	More
Cardamom	pungent, sweet	More	Some	More
Catnip	pungent	Some	Some	Some
Cayenne	pungent	Some	Less	More
Chamomile	pungent, bitter	More	More	More
Cinnamon	pungent, bitter	More	Some	More
Cloves	pungent	More	Some	More
Coriander	pungent, bitter	More	More	More
Cumin	pungent	More	Some	More
Dill	pungent	Some	Some	Some
Fennel	pungent	More	More	Some
Fenugreek	bitter	More	Less	More
Garlic	all but sour	More	Less	More
Ginger	pungent, sweet	More	Less	More
Horseradish	pungent	Some	Less	More
Hyssop	pungent, astringent	More	Less	More
Italian Seasoning	pungent	More	Less	More
Lemon Verbena	pungent, sour	Some	Some	Some
Lemongrass	pungent, sour	Some	Some	Some
Marjoram	pungent	More	Less	More
Mint	pungent	Some	Some	Some
Mustard	pungent	Some	Less	More
Nutmeg	pungent, astringent	More	Some	Some
Oregano	pungent	More	Less	More
Paprika	pungent	Some	Some	Some
Peppermint	pungent	Some	Some	Some
Poppy Seeds	pungent, astringent, sweet	More	Less	More

HERBS, SPICES	TASTE	VATA	PITTA	KAPHA
Rosemary	pungent, bitter	More	Some	More
Saffron	pungent	Some	Some	Some
Sage	pungent, astringent	More	Less	More
Spearmint	pungent	Some	Some	Some
Star Anise	pungent, sweet	More	Less	More
Tarragon	pungent	More	Less	More
Thyme	pungent	More	Less	More
Turmeric	bitter, pungent, astringent	Some	Some	More

NUTS, SEEDS	TASTE	VATA	PITTA	KAPHA
Almonds	sweet, bitter	More	Less	Less
Brazil Nuts	sweet	More	Less	Less
Cashews	sweet	More	Less	Less
Coconut	sweet	Some	More	Some
Filberts	sweet	More	Less	Less
Lotus Seeds	sweet, astringent	Less	More	Less
Macadamia Nuts	sweet	More	Less	Less
Mustard Seeds	pungent	More	Less	More
Pecans	sweet, bitter	More	Less	Less
Pine Nuts (Piñon)	sweet	More	Some	Less
Pistachios	sweet	More	Less	Less
Pumpkin Seeds	sweet	Some	Some	Some
Sesame Seeds	sweet	More	Some	Some
Sunflower Seeds	sweet, bitter	Some	More	Some
Walnuts	sweet	More	Less	Less

FRUITS	TASTE	VATA	PITTA	KAPHA
Apples	sweet, astringent	Some	More	More
Apricots	sweet, sour	Some	Less	Some
Avocados	sweet	More	Some	Less
Bananas	sweet, astringent	Some	Less	Less
Blueberries	sweet, astringent	More	More	Less
Cranberries	astringent, sweet	Less	More	More
Cherries	sweet, sour	More	Less	Less
Dates	sweet	More	More	Less
Figs	sweet, astringent	More	More	Less
Grapefruits	sour	More	Some	More
Grapes	sweet, sour	More	More	Less
Lemons	sour, astringent	More	Less	Less
Lemon, Orange Zest	bitter	Less	More	More
Limes	sour	More	Less	Less
Mangoes	sweet, sour	More	Some	Less
Melons	sweet	Less	More	Less
Nectarines	sweet, sour	More	Some	Less
Oranges	sweet, sour	Some	Some	Less
Papayas	sweet	More	Some	Some
Peaches	sweet, sour	Some	Less	Less
Pears	sweet	Some	More	Some
Persimmons	sweet, astringent	Some	More	Less
Pineapples	sweet, sour	More	More	Less
Plums	sweet, sour	Some	Some	Less
Prunes	sweet, sour	More	More	Some
Pomegranates	sweet, astringent, sour	Some	More	Some
Raisins, Currants	sweet	Less	Some	More
Raspberries, Blackberries	sweet, sour	More	Some	Less
Strawberries	sweet, sour, astringent	More	More	Less
Tangerines	sour, sweet	Some	Less	Some

BEANS, LEGUMES	TASTE	VATA	PITTA	KAPHA
Aduki Beans	sweet, astringent	Some	More	More
Black Gram (Indian)	sweet, astringent	Less	More	Some
Fava Beans	sweet, astringent	Less	More	More
Chickpeas	sweet, astringent	Some	Some	Less
Kidney Beans	sweet, astringent	Some	Some	Some
Lentils	sweet, astringent	Less	Some	More
Lima Beans	sweet, astringent	Some	More	More
Mung Beans	sweet, astringent	More	More	Some
Peanuts	sweet, astringent	Less	Less	Some
Pinto Beans	sweet, astringent	Less	Some	Some
Soybeans	sweet, astringent	Less	Some	More
Tofu	sweet, astringent	Some	More	Some
Split Peas	sweet, astringent	Less	Some	Some

DAIRY	TASTE	VATA	PITTA	KAPHA
Butter	sweet	More	More	Less
Buttermilk	sour, astringent	More	Less	Some
Cheese	sweet	Some	Some	Less
Cottage Cheese	sweet	More	More	Less
Cream	sweet	More	More	Less
Ghee	sweet	More	More	Some
Ice Cream	sweet	Less	Less	Less
Kefir	sour	More	Some	Some
Milk	sweet	More	More	Less
Paneer Cheese	sweet, sour	Some	Some	Some
Sour Cream	sweet, sour	More	Less	Less
Yogurt	sweet, sour	More	Less	Less

MEAT AND FISH	TASTE	VATA	PITTA	KAPHA
Beef	sweet	Some	Less	Less
Chicken, Turkey	sweet	Some	Some	Some
Duck	sweet	More	Less	Less
Lamb	sweet	Some	Less	Less
Pork	sweet	Less	Less	Less
Venison	sweet	More	Less	Less
Fish	sweet, salty	More	Some	Less
Shellfish	sweet	More	Less	Less
Animal Oils				
Eggs	sweet	More	Less	Less
Lard	sweet	Some	Some	Less

OILS	TASTE	VATA	PITTA	KAPHA
Almond	sweet, bitter	More	Less	Less
Avocado	sweet, astringent	More	Some	Less
Canola	sweet	Less	Some	More
Corn	sweet	Less	Some	Some
Coconut	sweet	Some	More	Less
Flaxseed/Linseed	pungent, sweet	More	Less	More
Margarine	sweet	Less	Some	Some
Mustard	pungent	Some	Less	More
Olive	sweet	More	Some	Less
Peanut	sweet	Some	Less	Some
Safflower	sweet, pungent	More	Some	More
Sesame	sweet	More	Less	Less
Soy	sweet, astringent	Some	Some	Some
Sunflower	sweet	Some	Some	More

SWEETENERS	TASTE	VATA	PITTA	KAPHA
Honey	sweet	Some	More	More
Lactose—Milk, Sugar	sweet	Some	Some	Some
Malt, Rice, Barley Syrup	sweet	More	More	Some
Maple Syrup (Syrup)	sweet	More	More	More
Molasses	sweet	More	Less	Less
Raw Sugar	sweet	More	More	Some
Rock Candy	sweet	Some	Some	Some
Sucanat	sweet	Some	Some	Some
White Sugar	sweet	Less	Less	Less

FLAVORINGS/ CONDIMENTS	TASTE	VATA	PITTA	KAPHA
Bragg's Liquid Aminos	astringent, salty	Some	Less	Less
Carob	sweet, astringent	Some	More	More
Chocolate	pungent, bitter	Some	Less	Less
Cornstarch	sweet	Some	Some	Some
Mayonnaise	sour, sweet	Some	Less	Less
Mustard	pungent	More	Less	More
Salt	salty	Some	Less	Less
Vegit	all	Some	Some	Some
Vinegar	sour	Some	Less	Less

BEVERAGES	TASTE	VATA	PITTA	KAPHA
Alcohol	pungent, sweet, bitter, sour	Some	Less	Less
Coffee	pungent, bitter	Less	Less	Some
Fruit Juices				
Citrus	sweet, sour	More	Less	Less
Other	sweet, astringent	Less	More	More
Herbal Teas				
Cinnamon,				
ginger, etc.	spicy	More	Less	More
Green, mint, etc.	astringent	Less	More	More
Milk and Dairy (see Dairy)				
Mineral Water				
(Carbonated)	bitter	Less	More	More
Soft Drinks	sweet	Less	Less	Less
Tea (Black, regular)	bitter, sweet, astringent	Less	More	More
Vegetable Juices				
Carrot	sweet, astringent	More	Less	More
Cucumber	sweet, astringent	More	More	Less
Spinach	bitter, astringent	Less	Less	More

INDEX

THE CHOPRA CENTER
FOR WELL BEING

Ginna Bragg and David Simon strive to fulfill their *dharma* at The Chopra Center for Well Being in La Jolla, California. The Center offers unique holistic health care and educational programs, which have been developed under the guidance of Drs. Deepak Chopra and David Simon. All the programs of the Center are guided by the principle that health is more than the absence of disease, but rather a state of dynamic harmony among body, mind, and spirit.

Ginna provides delicious, nutritious meals for guests and course participants at The Center and teaches inspiring weekly cooking classes. In addition, a wide range of workshops and seminars are offered through The Chopra Center for Well Being, including *The Magic of Healing,* an eight-lesson course to improve physical, mental, and spiritual well-being; *Magical Beginnings, Enchanted Lives,* a ten-lesson course for a conscious pregnancy; *The Healing Heart Program* for people facing heart disease; and *Return to Wholeness* for people facing cancer. Regardless of your current state of health, The Center is dedicated to raising your level of well-being and awareness.

For more information on classes and programs at The Center, write or call:

The Chopra Center for Well Being
7630 Fay Avenue
La Jolla, California 92037
(619) 551-7788

For information on healing-related seminars, books, videotapes, audio-tapes, CD ROMs, and products, call:

Infinite Possibilities International
(800) 757-8897

C O N V E R S I O N   C H A R T

American cooks use standard containers, the 8-ounce cup and a tablespoon that takes exactly 16 level fillings to fill that cup level. Measuring by cup makes it very difficult to give weight equivalents, as a cup of densely packed butter will weigh considerably more than a cup of flour. The easiest way therefore to deal with cup measurements in recipes is to take the amount by volume rather than by weight. Thus the equation reads:

1 cup = 240 ml = 8 fl. oz.   ½ cup = 120 ml = 4 fl. oz.

It is possible to buy a set of American cup measures in major stores around the world.

In the States, butter is often measured in sticks. One stick is the equivalent of 8 tablespoons. One tablespoon of butter is therefore the equivalent to ½ ounce/15 grams.

LIQUID MEASURES

Fluid Ounces	U.S.	Imperial	Milliliters
	1 teaspoon	1 teaspoon	5
¼	2 teaspoons	1 dessertspoon	10
½	1 tablespoon	1 tablespoon	14
1	2 tablespoons	2 tablespoons	28
2	¼ cup	4 tablespoons	56
4	½ cup		110
5		¼ pint or 1 gill	140
6	¾ cup		170
8	1 cup		225
9			250, ¼ liter
10	1¼ cups	½ pint	280
12	1½ cups		340
15		¾ pint	420
16	2 cups		450
18	2¼ cups		500, ½ liter
20	2½ cups	1 pint	560
24	3 cups		675
25		1¼ pints	700
27	3½ cups		750
30	3¾ cups	1½ pints	840
32	4 cups or 1 quart		900
35		1¾ pints	980
36	4½ cups		1000, 1 liter
40	5 cups	2 pints or 1 quart	1120

SOLID MEASURES

U.S. and Imperial Measures		Metric Measures	
Ounces	Pounds	Grams	Kilos
1		28	
2		56	
3½		100	
4	¼	112	
5		140	
6		168	
8	½	225	
9		250	¼
12	¾	340	
16	1	450	
18		500	½
20	1¼	560	
24	1½	675	
27		750	¾
28	1¾	780	
32	2	900	
36	2¼	1000	1
40	2½	1100	
48	3	1350	
54		1500	1½

OVEN TEMPERATURE EQUIVALENTS

Fahrenheit	Celsius	Gas Mark	Description
225	110	¼	Cool
250	130	½	
275	140	1	Very Slow
300	150	2	
325	170	3	Slow
350	180	4	Moderate
375	190	5	
400	200	6	Moderately Hot
425	220	7	Fairly Hot
450	230	8	Hot
475	240	9	Very Hot
500	250	10	Extremely Hot

Any broiling recipes can be used with the grill of the oven, but beware of high-temperature grills.

EQUIVALENTS FOR INGREDIENTS

all-purpose flour—plain flour
coarse salt—kitchen salt
cornstarch—cornflour
eggplant—aubergine

half and half—12% fat milk
heavy cream—double cream
light cream—single cream
lima beans—broad beans

scallion—spring onion
unbleached flour—strong, white flour
zest—rind
zucchini—courgettes or marrow